Collected Poems
2005-2025

Michele McDannold

ROADSIDE PRESS

Editor: Ezhno Martín
Cover Photography: Michele McDannold

Roadside Press
Meredosia, Illinois

CONTENTS

Stealing the Midnight from a Handful of Days

Notes on the American Apocalypse

By Plane, Train or Coincidence

Prose Poems

Stealing the Midnight
from a Handful of Days

#1

that maybe
if i just stand up
i can make a decision
that takes me
far, far away
from here
and where i've been
maybe
i already did
because sometimes
i swear
this is
all a dream
and in this dream
there is a fantasy
that is real
somewhere else
some other time
when we are
not just stealing
the midnight
from a handful
of days...

not recommended

this poetry is not recommended
for the young or bright-eyed
not recommended
for those weak in the stomach
or head
this poetry is not recommended
for the high-brow
sissified
punk bitches
who would turn a phrase
just to make you feel stupid
poetry is not recommended (period)
if you want to bury your head in the sand
and pretend the world is dying under corruption
we have a voice

this poetry is not recommended
for twitter or myface
you cannot like it
or share it in less than 140 characters
this poetry is not recommended
for nbc
definitely not the disney channel
we've got balls in our face
and dirt in our shoes
hot shit
red blood
cum stains on the inside pocket
there's a line in the sand that says go fuck yourself
anyone can do this
with enough guts and blaze
to set your ass on fire

an unnatural and often temporary absence

27 messages in the last hour
and i wonder if you could find me
in mexico

i wonder
how helpful it is
to have an epiphany
in your psychiatrist's office—
you are clearly insane
and your perspective
has been warped
for months now

right place, right time?

she asked me if this was
the same outfit
she wore last week
(how embarrassing)

i didn't tell her
i paid more attention to the line
of her bra
and imagined her naked
her soft curls
and
no, i didn't mention
or remember what she wore

"no matter what—
you have to be able
to like yourself,"
she says.

maybe canada,
i think.

they seem awfully pale
up there,
like me.

the phone rings.
time is up.
see you next week.

any day now

staring out
the psychiatrist's window
i see the wind
fucking with a tree
and a smokestack
shaped like a penis
a red, red sports car
the license plates say
MOROW2
i swear

what's green is green
the rest just looks
angry about it
spring is still
fighting its way.

monkey bars

isn't it
just a bit
usual these days
to be talking
shit, fuck?
i was reading this novel
by this great guy
'so and so,'
it was only
a few years back,
and it actually said
shit fuck,
shit fuck.
then later on
when i was reading
some other stuff—
poetry and the like,
well,
i had really
noticed
lots of cunts
for some reason.
i've never really
cared for that word,
and don't use it myself,
but back to shit fuck
it's losing power these days
it used to turn heads
even my mother
doesn't flinch anymore
when i let it slip
...fucking shit.

it started for me
on the playground,

a game with tracey,
the toughest girl in town
who i wanted to be
and jeff,
the dirtiest boy
in town
who i wanted,
even in grade 3.
man, don't tell me
we're not born with it.
so i learned all my
shit fuck
bastard, piss
on the monkey bars
but i never really
perfected it
until the year i worked
in that slaughterhouse.
i was nineteen and desperate.
everyone there was desperate,
shit fuck, became—
"i ain't takin'
no fuckin' shit
piss off, bitch
suck my dick."
it became
an art form
and second nature.
i know at times
you gotta keep it in check
and i do try
to tone it down
but damnit,
it's sewn deep
and when people keep talking
shit fuck, shit fuck,

sometimes,
i hate to hear others say it sounds cheap,
'cause baby,
it comes at a price.

too much

it was the adrenaline
it was the booze
it was nothing
it was everything
it's on the same page
as one sentence, only.
this is too much for me.

it's not leaving my room today
not answering the phone
or returning messages
this is just
the mind-fuck
i've been waiting for
in moments of
i.
don't.
care. about the consequences
it's live the dream
love so much
it hurts
like a bad country song
whatever it was or is
it should be worthy
of a sweet
but salty
jack & diet coke.

so white trash

i'm doing my best
to ignore the kids
but they are not cooperating
there is no peace
no quiet
there are only
moments of reprieve
when i can sink into the word
fall into a radiohead song
or two
or three
four or five
on loop

i'm a nervous mess
you are out of reach
and need more and more
to fill this new void

so i have
jack daniel's,
cigarettes,
coffee,
weed,
writing, writing, writing
the love letters
that will remain
unsent
the confessions
will stay locked up
hiding in the bathroom
sucking down a one-hitter

one of the girls

this one time
i stole the shoelace
of the girl
you were
fucking
down there
in your basement room

removed carefully
from one shoe only
ankle-high granny boots

and when it burnt
at midnight
it smelled of real leather
and lessons
i will
never learn

she was gone
the next week
with the others;
punk girls
pretty girls
nasty girls
reduced to receipts
and the occasional photo
maybe a ticket stub
a one-line tribute
in a poem
penned late night
at denny's
which will be remembered
long after

the curve of her ass or
the softness of her...

it is the sum of parts
you forget

crouched down
on the living room floor
surrounded by a circle of salt
the fire in my hand
and fevered head
i have nothing left to give
that you haven't already taken
and mixed in with the rest.

and now she goes by some other name

trina was
the skinniest girl
i had ever seen
hip bones
sticking out
pale
yellowish skin
and terrible hair
but she had a kindness
and mystical way about her
that was captivating

for a while
she was wiccan
a couple times
a buddhist
and always
with the tarot cards

she took me to my first
rocky horror picture show
we formed a coven
the boys brought flowers
mowed the lawn
wrote poems
sketches
long into the night
acid trips in the park
and no need
for explanations

the worst and most harmful
was her multiple personality disorder
i never really did buy it

it didn't really matter though
after the third abortion
when she told me
"i went into the bathroom
when he was done.
took that condom out of the trash
and shoved it up there."

one could fairly say
her mind broke then
in some abortion clinic
out west
where he held her hand
watching the light fade
right out of her.

disclosure

doesn't it just
suck shit
that i am not cool.
i am not the idea
of your black death love song
breathing demon blood in vain
but we don't sell happy juice here, either
got out of that business long ago,
i do believe in magic
and since i can find peace in that joy;
silly will do—
i think i'll be alright.

it's not so bad

i see her sitting
on the back steps
trying to hold her head up
with one hand,
a cigarette with the other

not a shower
or even a sink wash
it's been over 90 degrees
for a week
there's no electricity
no plumbing
hell, the floors are ripped out

a phone call
to the slum lord
and he says,
"oh yeah, i can fix that,"
but he never does...

the extension cord
hangs above her head
as she fingers the key
to the shed
in the back lot
where they store trash
that they pretend
is not trash:
bicycle pieces,
stained mattresses,
broken furniture
and on the side
that sits in the shade
a cage
with three bunny rabbits

she hands me a twenty
for the electrical cord hook-up
she says,
on sundays
the landlord
smells like fried bologna
but it's not so bad
she's had to do worse
to keep a roof
over her head

on a monday
she let the rabbits loose
but they kept coming back
to sit in the cage
with the door open wide

and i thought
it might make her sad
and i thought
it might drive her insane
suspended as she was
in a nightmare fairy tale
because i would,
i would find the sharpest knife
and release them all
for good

but she just sat there
continued to sit there
day after
shitty day
smiling
as if waiting
for a picture
to snap,
and the world
to go black...

i am a rock

of sea
of applesauce
of breath in the morning cold

i am a rock
broken and chipped
and weighed down to the bottom

sign of the apocalypse

he has pockets
and pockets
and pockets
suspiciously empty in the morning
and full at night
i'm pretending not to notice
the halo
that
in this light
is a bright neon blue
flashing
if you get close enough
(still pretending)
it says
open
Open
OPEN
goddammit
that's what i thought

i forgot

i forgot
how my phone works
i forgot
how to drive
how to go right on red
i forgot
to pick him up on time
i forgot
to take a shower
to wash my clothes
to stand,
walk,
be

i forgot my arm
in the other room
where it cooks,
cleans
and directs traffic
i forgot
to keep moving
in a straight line

basically
i just completely forgot
how to pretend
this is enough

i forgot
to hear the songs
to touch you
one last time
i just fucking forgot

i forgot
that comfort
can kill me
that contentment
will lock me up
and lose the key

i forgot
about grey skies
and cold rain,
puddles with nothing in them
but yesterdays.
goddamn it
how could i forget?

but i remember
i remember now
how to cry
i remember
all too well
this empty feeling
it's just that...
i forgot
how to live with it.

accidentally told you i love you

today i'm paddling back
to my lonely island
of, it's not that heavy
but the boat is sinking, fucker
oh, the boat is sinking

dear fucker

maybe it's okay just this once...

we live
with the choices
we make, shadows
in this fairytale
we're selling,
and walking a line
that is clearly
past the line
believing it's better
to pretend
not to notice

i'll tell you a secret
(no, i won't)

long gone
are the days
of low tides
and certain outcomes

the room
is a garage-filled cave
freezing
except for
the blue
blue
blue

when i reach for you
i reach
dreams
that live
in the breaking light

i have nothing
to lose
but this...

the sound—
a loop
of fingers
softly playing
this love song

sleep, you elusive bitch

my head is splitting
like dying
like murder
i can't decide which
and so maybe we should
go off in separate rooms
where there are no windows
and the temperature
is 10 degrees below
comfortable.

spinning lockstep

these streets
are transient
they ask
when will jesus
take your bitch away
they serve
to sup exploding lights
flying papers
of naked lady delights
day is night
is night is day
the autos just u-turn splash
but the soulless wear tags
professing a devotion to origin
st. louis, missouri
houston, texas
simply australia
return trip here or there
'cause anywhere isn't nowhere
after you've lived here
come rain or come shine
vegas is the vampire baby
worshiped not nursed
boned not begged
there is no virgin sacrificial blood
this is a hard-core fuck fest
you are worth one dollar
or a thousand or less
cents all translate into minutes
minutes of low-grade air
passing through the valley
just like the tumbleweed
spinning lockstep
over and over yourself

the big gulp

about living in vegas...
for the first three weeks,
we lived in a week to week
rental
it was—how shall i say,
questionable.

if you hear screaming,
do not come running.
happen to have a phone
call 911.
'course,
rooms don't come equipped
good luck finding a pay phone
with receiver still attached.

there was a pool though
there is not a hotel/motel/condo/shack
rental of any kind
in vegas that does not have a pool.
i think it's the law.
and, yes.
it had water.
and it was clean.
during the morning hours
when the bulk of the undesirables
were sleeping it off
or still kickin' it, but so fucked
they couldn't be of any real harm
i went swimming
it was bliss.

i don't care what anyone says
about dry heat

115 degrees
is 115 degrees
you sweat your ass off
it just evaporates so fast
it doesn't have time to collect
thank god for 7-11 and the big gulp
if it wasn't for the pool
7-11 and their big gulp,
99 cent shrimp cocktails
down on fremont street...
free spaghetti dinners
from that trashy casino
with the penny slots,
i never would have made it
those first three weeks.
i never would have hocked
everything i owned to stay on.

animals, every one of us

there was a lady found in dumpsters
all over town
spread by eight pieces of body parts
all but her head

it's at this point
i wonder if i might be
in over my neck

in the small towns
we keep our crime quiet
handle it ourselves
or completely ignore it
to the detriment of generation
after generation

wife beating
child molesting
occasional theft
or vandalism, drugs
nobody on the outside needs to know
unless of course
someone breaks out
moves on
then it usually goes
one extreme or the other
a victim—like that lady
or a victimizer...
animals, every one of us.

notes on world domination
(relevant is a safe word)

start with the death penalty
shoot-outs
marketing from the nazis

given over to indoctrination
american psycho
is cute
but cheesy
and does it better as
batman

the streets are not the same
i know

the smell of sweat is
everywhere
too much of anything
makes it mean nothing
and can sometimes kill you

there will never be another underground...

i found this poem in a notebook
(probably a manic fit)

find them a job with the chinese people!
i'm 3am on any bus outta here
taking my own advice dispensed,
ruffled and fluffed,
a little marked up
if she can take it
i can too
chain-smoking, poetry grenades,
bart rides
kentucky tea
crying
crying
laughing my ass off
the problems i have now are the
best problems i have ever had
i'm not even 40 yet.

better off dead

maybe i'd be better off dead
than sucking off these words
than percolating the hours away
with a slow-leak to your heart's last drop
maybe i'd be better off dead
than picking at my scabs
than erasing all the jobs i've done
with this broken-ass stub of a pencil
or maybe i'd be better off
deadly
cleaning my teeth with the shards of this thing
with a nice fat roll to my tummy
satisfied
and full
one last time, baby
hiccup

doorbells, mornings and death or (if you are cunt)

listen
when you start writing from the brain
chuck it out the door
feed the cats with it
call it meow meow chow
whatever
you've got to be heart, guts or balls
if you're cunt
you better know how to translate
and yes, they'll tell you to stop
and yes, they'll have all kinds of reasons and critiques and
blowhard bullshit
you might even believe for a while
it will throw you off
maybe you'll take on an old fat fuckin' mentor
start writing poems about doorbells, mornings
and death that does not
matter
and maybe everyone pulls a few chains now and then
and maybe everyone has a critic in their heart
and maybe not.
you could or could not say
'and' so much
it wouldn't matter
style has nothing to do with depth
and
if you shovel the shit long enough
you might forget what was under there
you might forget where you were going
you might forget how you were getting there
one day you'll remember
you wanted to go

you'll remember
earth doesn't taste like
dust
heat doesn't feel like
pain
and passion—

doesn't need to be developed.

empty pages

here is the paper
that taught me things
she has ability
she has potential
and an ink that comes to my skin
it fades
like the night
i like to see it coming on the morning
slow
with a tired and wrung-out feeling
it gives way to a new tension
this is the unknown
and i can write this
any way
i want

lost highway

this is the straight to hell version
your mother warned you about
an addiction
that you will serve
right up to the bitter end
when things have gone awry
many, many miles back

the top left open
the controls unmanned
one hour
in a roadside motel
at noon

there was a secret compartment
in the floor
off to the corner
where the carpet
was clearly cut

the place is clean
i'll give it that

the man at check-out
hands me a goofy smile
with a comment card
"everything okay?"
he asks
in his broken english

pausing too long
a moment here
could be disastrous
"yes, just fine."

i am on the lost highway
no cell reception
no rest stops
no one asking the wrong questions
and only one
thought—
linger.

#2

it was always there
right between the lines
subtle
sometimes, not so subtle
and if anyone ever saw it
i never knew
it's a hopeful sort of fear
standing on the platform
tracks, close
vibrating with approach
static electricity
there are many people here
but no one sees

so long as you let me take a nap

i'll stay up with you
push the boundaries
of whatever...
anything
i can't help it
this is realizing
where and who
you're supposed to be
at 6am
last stop, middle of nowhere
if you can resist
let me know how you did it
i have people and things waiting on me
and they may never come to realization
and i just might not care anyway
if you tell me it's alright
i will
believe

i'm such an asshole

not in the kitchen
not on my way
out the door
not upon waking
goddammit
will i think of you

i will not write
any more
sickening
gay rainbowing
it up
poems

only assholes
do that

a lifetime supply—

of gobstoppers
children with sticky feet
and no arms to cradle
your pumpkin head
you might be the first
in a long line of
rednecks
it's crystal meth
over sunday dinner
it's no longer barefoot
and pregnant
it's the latest 100 dollar plus
tennis shoe fad
selling your food stamps
for a purse dog
and a flat screen
it's a lifetime of fucking
and fighting
with nothing in between
but a protection order

this bored housewife

plots death by poison on odd days
mornings only
when the kids are gone
and the crock pot's set to high

cuts the hair from your head during the full moon
binds it with duct tape to a piece of ham
while the street is dark
and the dirt is warm

handles
rather than controls
the desire for witch-inspired zombie sex

this bored housewife
has a recipe book
that's time-locked
with a tequila switch
she's just waiting
waiting
waiting
til she can't anymore

fuck the holidays

something's burning
the house down
someone's throwing everything
out on the lawn

granny pissed the couch
and the other grandmother
had to go dry out
it's so mundane
who would bother
making this shit up

smells like
christmas
pledge furniture polish
and childhood disaster

joanna

she takes ass in the face during the week
in minivans parked on dark corners
on a tuesday night
1:43 a.m. to be exact

none to be the wiser
'cept she had phoned her friend
to say she'd taken
black nipple in her mouth

her husband later responds
oh shit
when told of the news
on the daily cell phone call

pulls his semi-truck over
to the side of the road
for a quick pull—
only to find himself crying
over the diseased cock
in his hand

this is how people with no skills get along in life,
so she tells me.

epic

my epic poem is a list of groceries
sorted by things i can buy
generic and not
the hero is a box of pop-tarts
because let's face it
nobody else can get the filling right

next to my bed
is the stepford wives
ear plugs
and a basket of lubes
lotions
and creams
for not having sex
for not looking younger
for not healing
the hole in my head

note to the better half

i miss the smell of mass deviation
of latino santa sweat
and artie's chronic 'n gun oil
i miss the pulse of drunk transit at 3am
black hookers in white wigs
and white pimps in purple satin
i miss the homeless junkies
and the rest stop houses
with sound systems
too big to fit
and fuckers too drunk to shoot, not fuck
i miss the rain that flooded my car
the stink that followed
and the body parts that washed up

yes, i miss being in love
on the run
and even pawning my only diamond
someday soon
there'll be a note void of tears
and dinners in the icebox
that freeze a lot better than i do.

they shared an identity of interests

i was given a line once
from a poem
i was told to take it into life
make it alive
make it a home
give it a new name
so there were sidewalks
running without shoes
those were cold on your feet
like an icebox empty of love
there was a tricycle
spinning wheels
faster than speed racer
take me on the back
i'll stand
and hold on
forever

the note from behind the stamp

if i am not in love
what can i tell you
there is not much left
worth
the ink

surprise, you're dead

i'm scared of my neighbor's eyes,
my landlord's tentacles.
wonder if this small-town life
is worth the low crime rate,
the faint smell of home
and knowing
all the streets
not by name
but a feel
rooted in twenty years ago.
taking the back road along the cemetery
there's a utility pole
with the words
"fuck life"
spray-painted
up the side.
it seems like the right place to be

and i am envious.

relief status

"there's a holocaust in my driveway,"
she tells me
a puddle of black
crude oil, that is
texas tea.

ask me a thousand ways, lady
the lies are the same...
relief status:
in process,
pending,
unknown.

i already know
she's fucked from here to
election day
at the very least.

a nice, quiet place

we don't have prostitutes,
crackheads
or faggots
hangin around the streets,
spreading their disease.

no niggers 'cept that one side of town.
when they shoot at each other—

we don't care.

we have more fast food places
than proper dining.
the walmart on the edge of town
is the place to be.

we like deep-fried, double-dipped
ignorance
served with a side of hypocrisy.

it's a nice, quiet place to live.
the criminals are advertised
in the newspaper and
on channel 2.
the real thieves

(of dignity, of justice
yes, those cunts)

they walk in plain sight.
at least they have the "decency"
to put their dogshit in a bag,
raise their flag high
and lock their guns up
at night.

god bless us,
everyone.

lolz

it's not my fault
i was born into
a redneck town
that hates niggers
and hides the innocence
of children
under a riverbed

poor, in a trailer
at a relative's
passed around
from one abuse
to the next

but i am not your victim
sorry, diet fads
sorry, dr phil
sorry, oprah

when you learn certain things too early
it fucks your head

the funniest thing i ever heard
at a poetry reading
was a rape poem

i expect neither of us
needs to apologize

dear baby jesus

thank you for the best childhood ever
for the nicely manicured lawns
dutifully tended to every Sunday
after church
for the sun tea baking on the porch
and the strawberries in the patch
thank you, baby jesus
for the community free of minorities
and forward thinking
for the streets free of gang violence
for the jehovah's witness even
and the evangelists
thank you for putting the shame on
all those unwed and/or single mothers
those people with the weak-minded mental illnesses
and the ghastly homosexuals
in general, just thank you so much
for putting a clamp down
on all the sex stuff
i didn't know what my period was
until i got it one day in gym

that kinda sucked
but thank you
and maybe while you were hiding
all the dildos and other adult fun
you could have taught the old people
not to stick their fingers and whatnot
in the young people
that would have been nice
but oh well
maybe that's why billy bob's uncle
is also his dad
i never met anyone conceived from incest before
coooool
thank you, baby jesus

i know. i know
some people want to give all the credit to satan
lucifer
the devil
whatever
he's busy with wars
tsunamis
and shit

he wants the glory of all those big fatality numbers
you...you are oh so patient
killing them softly and gently
with shitty lives
contrived of stifling rules...
call it morality!
shame, shame
the bent and twisted
call it love
baby jesus
i want you to have all the credit
saving us all from the fires of hell

i can pray to you for forgiveness
i can pray to you for the friday night football game
we can all join hands and pray pray pray
then sing the star spangled banner
oh, thank you, baby jesus
for making me an american
thank you for making us better
than every other nation in the world
so what if we drop the ball
in our schools
turn our backs
on mother nature
and would turn out
anyone or anything
in the best interest
of the almighty dollar

we are responsible for facebook
honey boo boo
and taco shells made out of doritos!
this is all thanks to you, baby jesus

but, wait...
i have more rights to my guns
than my own body!!
sweet baby jesus
thank you
oh, thank you
for women that know their place
in dresses
in kitchens
in the delivery room
children, children, children

let's have more babies, baby jesus!
every last one of them, precious
until they learn to breathe
in the polluted
but free as all fuck
liberty-laced air

everywhere, someone is dead

where are the living?
not down the street on the main stretch
packed into cars, stalling in traffic at noon
baked in the heat, counting
gallons of gas
burning more
and
more dollar signs evaporating
with the carbon
monoxide and food
money
gone, no
more money left
for medicine or the utility bill

forget school
forget resumes
nothing's left for you

the gap is ever widening

the forecast said 97
and mr. news reporter reports—
if you're not going over 45 mph
keep the windows down
you're moving too slow.

dick teasing is out of style

let's count backward from one thousand
and make pretty art slobber together
bedazzled eyebags
i cannot see
but no one else can either
let's smoke pot now
the day of the dead is near

the poets

they are too loud
yammering and bullshitting
poeticizing
but when they are gone
when it is quiet
i am empty

before the resurrection

i quit my job on good friday
i can't help it
that my sense of humor is kinda whack
and i believe that

shutting doors
is better than jumping out windows

the american dream

is a pair of pouty lips
stuffed in six inches of heel
i have excuses for flab that range from
silly
to
you can't dispute the benefits
of breast feeding
there's a shade of lipstick for that
and matching nail color
i figure i should quit smoking first
nicotine stains on fingers and teeth
but i will not lie
i love it
and do what i want
damn the consequences

that

is the american dream

i should pay my taxes

contribute to society
start a war
in my neighborhood
of lawn clippings
and garden gnomes
i wave at the neighbor
and he hates me right back

this quiet loathing
of property lines
and sagging trees
could put us both down

i already paid for my permission

at the food bank
it was expired cans of
fruit salad
and
stewed tomatoes

at the family resource center
there's a box in the back
where they keep the self-respect

pulling out my link card
at the grocery, in the checkout line
the lady behind me
wears a beautiful scarf
and a cute handbag
a cart full of fresh fruits and veggies
she's staring at my cheap,
overly processed boxes of food
and chunks of red meat,
my kid with his ipod...
she shakes her head.

at the social security office
their 500 question survey
about my schedule, my habits
and my inability to _____

it's the same everywhere
what you lack in money
you pay in your humanity

i jump up on the table in the junior high cafeteria
singing harper valley pta
nobody gets it
or laughs

i paid my dues
learned my lessons—

don't throw out those dented cans
the overzealous coupon purchases
don't throw anything away
i'm going to need it
i'm going to need all the buffer i can get
lest they take my overburdened soul
and recycle it for brownie points

i watch this game

from over here in my
little sandbox
it's a vantage point
i've come both to rely on
and suffer from
carefully construed moat
in case the barricade fails
it's high,
so i can barely climb
my rickety shit
to spy on this damn circus marauder
he is that one and she are all
the same
when i look close enough
their laughing looks like me too
it's just plain rude

a tired, diseased yellow

lost on the internet,
sifting through faces
i'm supposed to know—
the only witnesses to my lonely
and desperate choices.

i'm tired,
all too absorbed in the past.
this is an empty motel room,
reserved,
not paid for.

today

i only mean what i say
when i keep it to myself
it might be back alley logic
but it keeps my conscience clear

today it's raining
my heart pounds louder
than the drops hitting the roof tins
the sound of love, dropped
just shy of realization

i think of how easy it is
to get by
the cold night is near
you slip a bottle in my hand
and look at me like you're seeing yesterday

there is no tomorrow
and this, i keep
to myself

no malice intended

i fall, more often than not
just to the left of your shade
an empty bottle of spray
a used sandwich wrapper
the bottle cap
i'm below you, i know
from my vantage point, i see
though there are days i pretend
your swift kicks are
like the children, you are playing
as they do make a game of it

the raw egg and grits

the racial profiling in the kitchen is out of control
this man's voice transposes
the chords of hunter s. thompson
it's the violin's strings wiggling
slurs
i feel i've had too much
sugar
or otherwise
inactive ingredients
he is not wise
i suspect he thinks he is
talking loud enough to take pride
in absurdity
if you listen carefully
in the café
you can hear the
catfish growing
you can hear the
1963 ford
how it was
a maroon that resembled
the letting go of youth
you hear a groomed wisdom
sold over stories
well, some are true
and others are imagined so
something about keeping his coat shiny in texas
and how he says aaaa`
knows everything
about something
talks from a napkin
like the blood meeting air comes out blue
the words dribble out the mouth, tastes of poetry
shades that collide and fight for room
he says

if the cook is mexicano
he might understand the raw egg
even better
the black man
can't go wrong on the grits

aladdin's lamp

shouldn't have moments of realization in motel rooms
fake cups wrapped in plastic that they are
half-full, the cup ripped open
to serve my butt and ash turned to muck

every crook you ever knew hangs on these walls
pictures sold from black and white catalogue
half-wit, cutthroat competition
to sell their ass like the whore they are

and what have i done
lamplight burning 24/7
why bother with the clothes either
stacks on desks and tables of pizza boxes
not of novels or poems or papers

and the leaky window air conditioner says
buzz
buzz
buzz

café

we pick up from the streets, words
and skin stretched
thin over mother's lips.
dumpster love along the spillway, free;
sunshine through the way. she
dances to the jukebox,
a knife in back of cowboy lust
to celebrate the waitress.

open sign askew a door
of rust and nails of regret
scratchandspitandspew
coffee dust.

sloppy pasta

what if i said i didn't want to fuck you
not in yr agoraphobic lexicon pasty ego-trip
sweat pant adjective sideshow
what if i, then
said i loved most of your verbs but none of your nouns
how they looked de
pressed, sounded evermore like
doing the noodle
and it just won't stick, baby.
it just won't stick.

i'm coming to get your food

i'm thinking of moving
perhaps i will go
where there is a good
food pantry

being poor is a matter
of shifting
shifting things around
until things get better

las vegas, nevada
population 478,434
does not have
a desirable food bank

back in '95
i open'd up a package
of dry blueberry muffin mix
with much excitement
i dumped 'er in the bowl
and cracked
my eggs right in

(those were some of my last
few cents—those eggs.

no eggs at the food pantry
and groceries don't come cheap
in the land of endless buffets)

i stirred like i hadn't eaten in days
because *i hadn't eaten in days*

dipped
my fingers into the batter

for a taste test
just before she reached
my tongue, mouth agape
my eyes spotted the tiny mealworms
swimming
around the mixing bowl

DAMN!

my finger
the bowl
my finger, the bowl

eyes darting back and forth
should i?

god, i am *so* hungry.
protein,
right?

how many times had i heard that
accidentally swallowed a bug
—didn't kill me. i'm still alive.
still standing here.
but, for how friggin' long...

FUCK!
[splat]
(blueberry-worm wall food)

note to self:
thank food pantry for pine-sol—
quite handy in dining room

yes, the smaller towns
though, not too small
they get the better stuff

fresh stuff

they get all society
and competitive
about their food banks
like
jacksonville, il
population 18,940

you can even get fresh bakery goods
on certain days.

it's the bomb.

criminally speaking

i'm considering one of those robberies
where they drive a truck through a
convenience store
and take off with an a.t.m.
but i'm too lazy, old and broken for this
a criminal by definition
cheating welfare
driving without insurance
stupid poor shit like that
i don't have the balls for serious drug abuse,
highway robbery
or even jaywalking
my crime is denial and safety
as i type these words
i'm already fingering the delete key

something in the way

so many w/ great hair
and bad eyesight
if the moon
were a spork
well, ya know
even the cat is sick of it
there is nothing
but to sleep
to grind
to slide forward
to be
a lightning bug
smacked to the windshield
glowing bright
for one more
moment

nothing to lose (or freedom)

i need to be
that guy...
the next one in line
as the door closes,
the last one picked,
the "we just sold out"
of every kind of whatever
you're looking for,
the flat tire,
the flat busted...
left for dead,
fucked over six ways
to sunday,
guy.

that guy whose lover
stole a pigeon heart
and took a big dump
on his head.
fuckery, so insane
so very needless...

all reason, if there ever
was any—
is totally obliterated.

i
want to be that guy

"that kind of pissed that leads not to revenge
but to a reckoning"

people will shed a lone tear
sniffle
and shake their head a lot

i will keep on gathering great poems
sharing the news about great poets
new ones
old ones
killer ones
fucky ones
we'll call it
the "didn't make it to twitter
because it had too much
character" book

i want to drive down the great river road
i want a reading
right now!
in bars
bookstores
and bowling alleys
i want to read/scream
at bikers and rednecks
housewives and whores
i hope they throw stuff
and spit on me
chase me out to the car
yelling
"we don't like your kind
'round here"
but they will secretly
worship me
and my freedom
and my hoard of poets
from the suburbs
the city
the farm
they're multiplying like gremlins

one dash of sit and spin
and they're out ruining christmas

i want them all
(not to make them famous)
to make them infamous
to spread their disease
of think
of cut out the bullshit
and get to the point
i want america
in her glazed over red bull eyes
to really
really
wake the fuck up
this is no time to let it ride
the great depression
is your brain on ice
your investment in image
the "i'm okay—you're okay" is a dead hippie lie
the 1% is selling everything
is selling you, me..
mcdonald's and twilight books

medication via
tv ads
the party is over
the beatniks are dead or dying
the outlaws are a joke
the wild west is tamed, my friends
rail against that which seeks to defeat you
every day
every hour
right now
get in your car
go
don't kill the first thing that gets in your way
kill em all
kill em all
kill em all,
motherfuckers.

they call us the X generation
with nothing to lose
but our nirvana cds
and fight club on dvd
didn't you get the memo?
the *they* have

co-opted your identity for mass marketing
you can now buy
the special edition director's cut t-shirt snuggie toothpick rim job with
decal

get the fuck
out
out of your house
and stick a fist up their ass for doing this
don't buy the hype
use it against them
like those goddamn
nothing to lose
asshole poets
that you love

flowers, mostly plastic

in the back yard
i had a big mound of sand
two times, maybe three, my height
supposing to play in
sometimes i even did

building castles, forts and things
more often than not, i sat on the edge of the yard
where there was a plot of concrete
planned once for a basketball court, i think

there i would sit
on the cool cement among the abandoned,
rusting metal toy cars
and watch

i was watching the wind blow
and the shadow fall
i was watching every tiny distracting sense
of the moment
as it passed
in the graveyard next door

i watched the people come, though not often
i watched the flowers, mostly plastic
i watched them fall and tumble
i watched them scoot, almost play
one day here, another there
among the gravestones
i watched the seasons change
the leaves on the trees to the ground
and the man working

i would hide then, behind the shed
watching in secret

how do they care for their dead?
(i did not think of that then)

bittersweet

you're walking barefoot on the last day
of your forever summer
too damn cold
to feel the asphalt melt into
the wind
smiling
the way you smile
before the frigid air
takes the something
that's been in your skin for so long

how to be born-again and feel alright about it

get too drunk too fast
close your eyes and spin spin spin
where's the weed?
he's laughing in my ear
and i'm hiding from the other room
this is normal, right?
jesus was a baby and always will be
temporary alcoholism
permanent un-inhibition
water saves the day

rubber white and puckered

i dreamt of living in a rubber room
(my head wrapped around a train)
the whistle
it doesn't sound like a whistle
not like the old western movies

when i say old
(i mean dead, they seem dead)
that black and white trapped in a box
must be bones
it is similar to the pale mornings
when i visit the mausoleum
in the back where the tiles pull out

no one comes here anymore
not to see the picture behind glass that was sampson
that was julia
they don't notice a dead bird brought in from the rain
no

the tiles are white
all else is ash grey
black
the train sounds
a horn
a horn that won't let up
on and on it goes

as it reaches the end of my mind
the sound fades
end of the track
the last stand of town
the sound of the rails
the rumbling

a vibration
rattling windows

there are no windows here
only rubber
rubber white and puckered
[in the room, we are back in the room]
with buttons
small, round
it looks like a couch

all the way round the room
(you can find death in rooms too)
you can see the door is the outlined shape of a door
sticks out from the rest

it feels like i could run
run into it
and the sound
the sound might go away

#3

i'm not going to torture you with this
loving down to the bones
what we have
is impossible
and yet somehow
true
for every person that
came back from the
brink
throw me a
line
before i sink
completely

what else?

we seek
the limits of oblivion
the arms
secrets
and unveiling
we are
to our detriment
laughing

the facts and details

at some point
you'll start to wonder
where i left you
and went with those other men
i start to think
and smoke some more drugs
what is the difference
between
instructions and directions

you won't want to know
his arms worked better than yours
in holding me down

your mouth is the lack of,
i dream—
still...

rinse,
repeat

veer right at the curve
if you have to crash
go to your right
if you have to

this highway leads to
this highway
and nothing else

8 horrible ways the universe can destroy us

and they happened without warning

the fade
the cut and run
the never was what you thought in the first place
the dry, sucking ache of just not right
the disconnect
the gray the gray the gray

it's about
cutting things down
to the quick
something that
happens
without warning
when you think
too much
& hold it in

i apologize in advance
your metaphors

are like
a sandbag
in a desert

today
is the
beginning
of the end

i have already cried enough

find a way

find a way to be invisible
flesh-colored
costume
that blends well
with the starless night
your hand on my mouth
i feel nothing now
goodnight dots
goodnight cursor
blinking
a safe word
with a stranger is
yes.
goodnight love
deconstruct this poem
in the morning

cemetery poem (for my love)

i'm sitting here at the
cemetery
talking to myself
i think i'll probably
be here a while
be doing this
wondering all along
if it will be enough

this is where i go
when none of it makes sense
just so you know

where it is quiet
my mind quiets
there is some sort of peace
in the finality

i think of papa
his letters
sent home while
out on the river
or out to sea
for months
and months on end
starting the letter, stopping
and beginning again
if only a sentence or two
in between the work
that keeps him away

how he called her
my love
and still she
drank just a little too much
a little too often

all this i learn from old letters
see in yellowed photographs

how she stared off-center
with a sadness around
the eyes
only laughing in the photo
when he's seated next to her
and all those years
since she died
he lived on, puttering
through life
i wonder if he
pretended she was there
for the rest of it
for the baseball games
over the radio
the mornings in the garden
the looking out over
everything
wondering...
what does it matter
anyway

today on duncan avenue
in diamond grove cemetery
it does not matter
i talk to myself
i will lie down
in the earth by myself
search for you
in the next life
and hope
it will be easier

Notes on the
American Apocalypse

shaken not stirred

it got all blurry on me
misty, wheezing stuff
puffing up, nauseating

you can survive on
coffee and cigarettes
it just hurts sometimes
when a deep breath whistles
through your chest

oh, hell
i had to squint to pop that bic
the flame quivered
choreographed hallucinations
tippy-toe dancers
in a tangerine ballet

there's nothing like the rush
to my achin' head
my java syrup
black divinity
and shakin's just a state of mind
i mind sometimes

in the consideration of john

i felt he was insecure
as he did often call me names, though
i caught his glances at my budding breasts. then
there was that time in the public pool when
he brushed up against my flesh, and
he smiled at me so dashingly.
yes, i would say dashingly—like
a movie-man, a
bogart, or
today's edgier nicholson, but
it quickly turned his
scooping me up, and
a toss.
i'll never forget
the bleeding.

ode to my lips

let me introduce you to my
lips.
bloated, red things they are
plastic, wet dipped in paint.
lost in artistic rendition
of a perfect kiss.

i'll test your sense ability
to perceive
where men have wept at flesh,
(wrapped around) crooked.
morsels gobbled up like sweets;
then flung away with their semen,
their soldering irons on lax skin.

oh, there were odes to the scoundrels.
demands for explanations challenged
our justifications, trespassers.

call me a tramp.
you'll love me—
a snake that calls itself a tongue.

forget the vacation, it's time to fumigate

i will push and push
just to hide there, dear.
always in the fresh scrape
of flaky skin dust.

when i pretend it's fun,
you'll look on.
i know too well;
i've seen those eyes.

the decline has been on
for weeks now.
you half expected it—
no; you hid like turtle doves.

out in the garden,
you go slow,
and hope it stops
the time.
i avoid the room
we share.

apollo must have his way with me,
summer's here.
pollywogs and earwigs have crawled out
and stay.
i just can't explain...
you never quite understand
where the strings go in my head
to loopy loop land.

the performance

everything important is hidden
like keys in a latch, all broken
deep in my womb, now empty

to say that words go in circles
say it

forever looking in cameras
talking

contractual terms
always a cliche to explain it
or bear it

it's expected to make it better
like a visitation
(velvet reds—couches, black dresses)
i've tired
of standing in lines
shaking hands
mouthing words of assurance
        "it's okay"

as good as it gets
goes a long way to explaining
(that is, to truly minimize)
this day-to-day dance

if you won't play along
i'll have to cut you
out, that is
the show must go on
you know
over the years
i've learned
how to go on
on with the show

to say that words go in circles
say it

on smoke and mirrors

the movies are always liars.
you can't type with a cigarette
dangling from your lips for long.
well...you can, but there's no point.
if you inhale, you get smoke in your eyes.

corroded arteries

i swear it;
momma sucked on hitler
under the christmas tree.
i saw it;
he was grinnin' from
knob to nose hair
under the twinkly lights.

i would have missed it all,
if it hadn't been for grandma.
it started with the
usual carol burnett,
and the ear...
always the yanking
of that ear.
then, on to the good stuff.

i think it was that movie
with dennis hopper.
the one with the vagina rape,
that glass bottle thing.
at least, i think it was dennis.
or maybe it was that
scar-faced guy,
with the people at the end of the street,
or the top of the hill.

whichever it is,
they were having sex on the beach...
and rubber boats filled with
marijuana,
the cliffs—
there were sacrifices
of virgins to great stone gods.

i got the horror flicks
and the b, sex-pot movies
of the 80s
smooshed together
like meringue pie
and saran wrap.

late nights with johnny had
not quite prepared me
for this evening's show.
though, ed mcmahon laughing
always sounded a bit like
satan coming.

bettin' man

it's when you realize
you're in the small percentile
that has no chance—
that gets the closed-door
treatment
from the doc.
come in,
take a seat;
(with soft hands)
as you're sitting there,
all you see is
bobbing heads
        bobbing heads.

your ass has puckeered
        puckered   so tight.
you've just ingested your best whitie-tighties
cotton for air,
as the sweat comes pouring once
        comes pouring forever
at night and forever.

you laugh at rumble bees

it's not hard to skip the meals,
shuttle around with caffeine,
but today there's a window shop
of sweet rolls and honey buns
scrooge counts the saccharin drops.

throwing a rock in the beehive,
it's the sound i hear under this
overpass, over and over again.

you laugh at the rumble of bees
when the tables are empty,
no humans chawing foods,
no one to bring you the smell,
or remind you of the texture.

you can almost forget the way
your lips have become chapped,
cracked—

the impression is worn away,
a sensation ground out to grit,
such flippant thoughts as yourself.

these abstentions make you impotent.
you can't taste the snot that rolls down
into your mouth at instant intervals
from that head cold you developed.

the tears, though...
...you can almost feel
the salt on your tongue.
i mean, feel it.

you want to wrap your tongue around it,
covet the thing, hide it,
and you never really knew what
bittersweet tasted like til just now,

as you remind yourself—
every experience has its
pearl.

message board mala

mental :stability
reading the   dsm for hobbies
a round   of pogo
with invisible   electro-super heroes
a rather encour aging convolut-in' conversation
with the delete button
delete .button

ahhhh!

she's the latest 'it' girl
followed by a round of
needle kept, pen tapped
junkie monkies

well, it sounded good
all around about
2:43 a.m. at the local
bleeding joint

which is just down the hall
in her sitting room
a cross-legged meditation
in banana suits

with a keyboard jolt
for good measure
and all the letters
she licked them off

while the whole crowd
just went
awe

that thing you call sleaze

imagine that, please.
spare me the one more night
wet dreams poet fantasies skimmed
off factory sweat and tired knees.
you sound just like a bunch
of fucked-up pollinatin' bumble
bees trapped in a jar of their own
honey comb design and man-made
disease. get off your plateau of
circle-jerk tease, i'm so sick of that
slap-ass rim-hole condition that you
call sleaze. if i gotta go down on your
crooked cock called pen one more time—
baby,...please!

the coupling

she is moist
she is deep, down dirty moist
she is the finger waiting
just above that whole of love

he is hard
he is brick, bound beatin' hard
he is the pocket open
only before the final crush

things you learn when not looking, but looking

i always chose vidalia onions
as my mother did
though i opted for chopping
rather than criss-cross, saw

i shave my legs, daily
as she did
mine are a bit longer
thicker, but firm
my breasts are bigger
always did remind me of melons
hers i thought, prettier
like pearls

i wonder
what my son
will glean from onions
will he come up vidalia
or will it be
yellow, white, or
maybe even purple

let go my black hole, stephen

rapt,
in my gogo vintage green
hearse
i realized i had stopped living.
this pulse, this heartbeat—
what did it mean?
synchronicity,
the radiation technologician,
snappy, white coat
with a flirty, black line
up the back fishnet
suggested—
it was simply organic.

...the radio played
the blues brothers
the blues bros.
soulman
soul man
something of my spirit
had slipped away, unnoticed.
(danny, where are you?)

...what was all this
brain function?
staring only makes you sweeter,
perspective for body bags
ripe for mind fodder.
tag
tag
you're it
because i'm thinking about it.

could it be only a misfire,
random shots of electrical juice—

fire flooding the synapse?
is it just white noise
flying under the radar?
redundant,
redundantly,
repeating,
regurgitating.
mushroom clouds—
could you find a bunny
floating, pink-eyed
and wild?
[thought-police]

—a 1950s
stepford-head code.
was it all loud enough
that i did not hear myself
saying goodbye?

midsection

i quit smoking once
or thirty times
it's all the same really
well, this one time
it was the bloody filters i quit
the smell of them bastards
when burning, made me gag
this girl i was living with rolled her own
she had a bright yellow head
so i tried
it always came out so fat
in the middle
kinda like i was becoming
and becoming i was
it was the baby, you see
roley-poley
it felt like butterflies
flitting around soft blue clouds
and pink flowers
'cept for the gagging
we would have just kept on
with fields and rainbows
yeah, occasional puke
but for the brown head spike man
that kept coming with his moon pies
and promises
should've left the chain on

doin' tussin

there is a beat box, baby.
i found it in the basement.
it goes—
when we do robitussin
by the bottles.
it responds primary colors,
flashing (*.*.*.*)
to janis joplin, mostly.
but, these days
i like ministry.

...and so i,
kick it
with my
combat boots,
when i can't
find a vinyl
in the crate
to
get you
off.

do not alarm yourself

the couch is burning on the front lawn.
it was a pretty blue.
now, it is ravishing,
the kind of blue that is silence.
it is consumption.

the old one—
well, it was
powder-puff.
there were tiny white flowers,
so small.
i'm not sure what kind.
these were accompanied
by specks of beige,
nondescript skews,
all quite pleasant enough.

the flames in granite city
pulled the car to a stop.
sometimes things are so
cliche you begin to
understand why.

lost so far from everywhere
and the road empty of anything,
but you.
though there had to be
tens, hundreds,
working...
that concrete monstrosity,
somewhere in the bowels
of those giant towers,
at the bottom of those stacks,
keeping it roaring,
surviving the stench
of burning gas.

could they see the flames
from down there?
could they see what i see
from over here?
on this lonely patch
of deserted highway,
middle of the night,
awe-struck.

blue light—
freak out.

i can smell the
noxious perfume
reaching across the
barren fields.
yank the breath from
my own throat,
my own nostrils.
the hand is never quick
enough.
pinch my nose,
cover my mouth,
but my lungs feel
tainted.

here i stand, in the
front yard,
sucking it all up.
i take a deep breath,
tilt my head back,
close my eyes and
exhale.
sometimes the burn
is just a part
of you.

rookie and the world

i just need help when i want to grab something
were you blind or were you stupid
i'll never know

rookie
and the world
quickly turned from juicy fruit
to adams sour apple

i look at how often we're similar
across maps, photos, cables, words
i draw lines—connecting
sounds to make you shiver!
i put an X there
Bloodcurdling!
Terror!
Horror!
(in) stereo

but, more so than i see you
i saw myself once
floating above an open me
stuck like a pig on the conveyer belt
and the line was shut down
and the men and women working there
they were tired of that
they were tired of that line shutting down
for whatever reason up ahead
for whatever didn't matter
they wanted that line to go
they wanted that piece of meat right there
to get cut
get bagged
get boxed
and get out

but, this is the nature of things here.

i have the whole world now
like a reincarnation
it's good to be born-again.

six miles from graceland

i imagine it could be better
but like so many things
it's just dust on the shelf
collecting
all these sounds and vibrations
simply irritate
my already abrasive mood

we were six miles from graceland
when a familiar snort belched
from the chassis of our carriage
number three, as i counted,
on my list of three things
that go wrong in succession—
check.
yes, check engine light is blinking
orange madness
i can only exhale puffs of
yellowed smoke
hold it back a moment
form the perfect O
and drive through the destruction
of this engine

i've an appointment to keep
and though i may not know the way home
i have seen the signs already
and so i will creep-crawl
pray on everything holy
and call on everything dark
maybe i will get there

when i arrive
they will pull back the ropes

and i will sing
straight string black
on crushed purple velvet
melted with baroque, babe
liquid liberation

welcome home

it is never quite what you expect
the skip-a-long gives you the push
to the west
a head's down to the
righteous man's poor land

today there is no hot water, sir
perhaps tomorrow we will bleed out
some heat for you

a little here
a little there

increments of warmth
of worth
there are tags on the walls
gang signs
scratches on the floor
a boy carved out his name
to say—i was here

it is only the big man that can wash
away the sins of a slum lord
...the sands of time to carry away
the lost

never say die

do not die by the words
die by the cunt
or the cock
this is not love
love is non
yeah, just that
and so the conclusion
getting over yourself
into the real self-loathing debauchery
if you can find a trick that gives you no worry
you can smile your way out
and die with a good one in your mouth

not like the movies

i went down to see what was going on, as
if i didn't know, well
maybe more to confirm that
all was as the world goes.
if the faces change,
the people stay the same.
they still know who i am—to
who i am in the scheme of things.

j—
j, i said.
you are out of your element, i explained.
yes, yes...she breathed—(through her eyes).
i heard tell of it in the movies, though
never seen it done in real life, and
in a place like this, well
it didn't seem very wise.
i was afraid the smoke in the air
might vaporize her head.
she touched my face with her
little hands, said
come with me,
then i knew it was bad,
worse than i thought.
i found a barstool to hide behind,
a key to send her away with.

now and again, in a quiet, empty moment,
i think about her unwearied commitment
to a slow and lonely death.

alphabet entrance

take me away, silly puppet
dangle in front of me
a thousand symbolic fonts

mary

in a frame, i would call unfortunate,
picked over by the color-blind.

the print falls away, warped.
did you see it falling?

mary comes.
mary licks her fingers,
then touches,
then licks some more.
mary feels small.
mary understands
the swift, exacting
death of a small thing.

smoke

i only saw
an artifact
leaning against
a light pole
a few tattoos
on muscled sleeves
working down
a cigarette
a masterful ace
with the smoke
how it rolled
across the most beautiful
lips
fingertips played
a flicker game
disposing of ash
though somehow
motioned erotic

tried writing a poem

first line—i'm still a romantic
i guess the quota for bullshit
is full up
for the day

it might be true

i wonder how
the fly gets
into the room.

into my head
wormy words
like noodles
and gross
and sucked up
through my nose

they make my eye hurt

my son says
"flies puke on everything
they land on."

i forget myself—
smile
we talk about frogs that disappear
land on the other side
of the country

mid-day
shining sun
as surprised as everyone
they are there

the packinghouse—second shift

beyond the gray gates
a soft sweet spot
remembered.

i put my hands
on the dead
cut flesh
that was.

it is my job
to bag the familiar
clear plastic,
soft pink
flesh
so cold
so very, very
cold.

we move swiftly
through the process.
do not think
of the dead,
but of babies,
men
the rent
heat...

living on main street

we fuck
in front of
the big window
at 2am
the traffic
outside
steady,
but slow
some drive by
twice

pretty things

i used to blow up
plastic lighters,
it's really quite easy,
not very dangerous,
except for maybe
to the fingers
and maybe
any nearby
flammable
items.
it starts off spitting
little droplets
of flame
like baby
roman candles,
only not so
big.
kinda pretty.

let loose a natural language

she often forgot the sound of intelligent.
she gawked at orange things,
marveled at the brashness of it all,
construction signs,
the harvest moon,
a basketball,
on some silly afternoon that
paled next to blue
and oceans of salt shakers
and pillars from sex cursed and stoned.
always back to the stories sold on morals
backed in blood.
the tablets said it all.
in pieces, they hummed
to the tangerine orb,
the gut-wrenching howl
of an unleashed thing.

an empire

we were mothers
of sons to be kings, the leaders.
    it was armageddon
brought it down.

what were you thinking?
huddled 'round the table,
the times we talked of mountains
all the noise of revolutions,
    how we
hashed it out.

was it something in the dick we had
when we were children?
...or the trailers,
    the common threads
binding us.

raised in metal shacks,
some sort of conduit,
a combination of the two—
metal and dicks.
    one to bring it down
one to put it in.

it's just coincidence
your boy can't grow hair.
it's not...
it's not the end of the world.
we would go in hum-vees,
or maybe atvs.
scared to death my boy
    would die, miss
his prophecy.

we were sure it was mountains,
canada.
there's proof in it.
after the survival, left alone,
a tribute in a chair made to rock
it soothes,
      arms wrapped
(around.)

we needed it—
we saw it, desired it.
      so they brought it.
on their shoulders, in a waft of fire—
by their hands, our kings.

this has been a recording.

you will really like me
once you get to know me.
just don't ever
agree
to meet me
in a dark alley
or a side alley
er...
any kind of alley, really
have you ever heard of ocd?
since we're setting the ground rules here
let's just agree
to keep it out of the streets, entirely
also,
don't let's ever meander
into burger king
for a late night thing
me and the king
go way back
and it's kind of a
thing
as like
in the trigger way,
and i might feel
the need to
deep fry pickle your ass
also,
while i'm thinking about
that particular incident
don't ever follow me
into a bathroom
no matter how much
cajoling there is
no matter if
there's something in my eye

something in your eye
or your girlfriend's eye
just go straight
to the emergency room
send me on to walgreen's
for some iodine
plan ahead
send your brother
to keep me company
i don't mind brothers
and brothers don't mind me
it's the perfect kind of company
somehow, people get this silly notion—
ocd is like counting light switches and door knobs,
a dozen egg cartons and washing hands till they throb
what a bore
but seriously,
if i show up on your door-stoop at 3am
with a bag full of nothing and a shit-eatin' grin
you might as well
let me in
or call the cops
whichever scene
you think you can
tolerate
the most

a private vacancy

i take the window seat
as we drive away
from the tourist town
searching the roadside
for a motel

i secretly yearn
for the seedy
underbelly,
the $30
no-tell motel
where the
softly swaying
neon sign
screams
Vacancy.

they don't check
id.
you are no one,
anyone,
every one.

only two things
get done
in these places,
violence
and sex,
sometimes
both.

these are the
nasty details,
i've alluded
to you—

the tiny bit
of spit i left
behind your ear,
the questions
i see
in the
grey flecks
of your eye...

i swear,
in the set
of your jaw,
in that bar
where we met
on that night
in our town.

we knew.

don't you know?
you, don't know?
about me.

when we check
into our $95 room,
carefully—i pull away
the bedspread.

"they never wash
these things."

depending

maybe i'm too old
for hard luck stories
figure it's 'bout the choices you make,
the life you lead...
turns lady luck hot or cold.
she can be a bitch.
you decide who serves who
...and your glass—
it really is half this
or half that,
depending.

tip of her finger

she said his love is heavy
brilliant
and savage
speaks with a poet's tongue
smiles
in ways she never knew
hides her things
in cabinets
behind glass
using tricks
to sneak it all away
afraid of the small cut
on the tip of her finger
that never heals
that's one in a million to him
surrender a thousand times a day
to his kiss

the process of decay

when we were kids
we played with popcorn, unpopped
the girl down the street smuggled it out
contraband
in her little hand, she doled it out
it was bigger than mine
hesitant though, i followed

eat this and wait
—the end of the explanation

spin...and spin...and spin

at 8:00 they'll turn off the lights,
the fridge will go hot,
the air-conditioned rooms,
knocked off by blankets,
nurtured by fans—
gone.

the men in the trucks
will come—
all out of red tags.
they've given us fair warning.
today is the day
and i've nothing to do
but sit out back,
watch the meter spin,
wait for it to stop—
hope, somehow
the bill
will get paid.

who died and made you a shoe

the bird is singing
the beauty is in the air
is in the still
is in your pants
but you're e.d.
ashamed to buy a little blue pill
called roxie
down the street
in the wrong bar
is the right girl
she has no teeth
but will tell you there's a sunnyside
to
everything

it happens.

i've been reading
the same damn book
for ten years
on and off,
over then over again.
i pick it up,
then put it down again;
much like the man
who gave it.

submit here

5-8
sounds like a good stretch for robbery
minus the weapon
and not a guideline
i search my pockets for both
and find only
a lighter,
a ponytail
and some lint.
it was easier when i had
less to lose
and more to believe in

claire

works at her desk
takes meetings at her desk
eats lunch at her desk
occasionally cries
at her desk
she's walled in by books—
training manuals
neatly arranged chaos
her religion is both a purpose
and a comfort
where family, friends and coworkers
have failed
a smart pair of shoes
have never let her down

the dead road

she is dead
circles life
like flies to shit
her body, a temple to nothing
gut from children
that left her heart
long before
they left home

she is dead
walks the road
of lower middle class
zombies

there are no
mean streets
in this town
only sad
glossed over
cul de sacs

she is dead
knows the way
when the signs fall
and go rotten

private
no way out
dead end

POEMS TO CELEBRATE MY FRIENDS, PEOPLE I KNEW OR HEARD OF, AT LEAST ONCE, AND THEN THEY DIED OR WILL DIE AND I WANNA BE PREPARED (in 3 parts)

1.

stop sucking on todd moore's dead dick

ode to the bullet-wielding
gangster
dillinger dogma
poems i don't get
but ur take of them
is worse
or ur take of him is worse
i guess
i never knew him
or you
but feeling fully qualified
to pass judgement
in poetic form
i find it
sickening
pathetic
and sucking his dead dick
well,
it's just in bad taste
(end poem)

2.
the corpse of tim murray

still has reddish hair
and wears glasses
like heaven in a cup
smells like pumpkins
and whip cream
don't judge me for
sniffing his sweater vest
i'm lost on the highway
between popesville
and agnostica
broncho john
is weeping

3.

when you're gone

let there be hamsters for all
and depends undergarments
just in case
may there be poetry grenades
sloshing around the room
til we're all sloshing
to that private tune
that drives danny's big banana
i have never sent a poem that rhymes
to anyone else that matters
and when you're gone
i still won't tell
that one secret
but i can't speak for that
guy sleeping/not sleeping
on the chaise lounge
he
will probably tell

afternoon forensics

"I don't believe in accidents. There are only encounters in history. There are no accidents."—Elie Wiesel*

how clusters become clusters
a piece of gum wad
bright green
something foreign in that—
black

how toilet tissue, when wet
is surprisingly
twistable
makes a neat, long roll
as when we messed with play-doh
in kindergarten
but without colors

a round, bright red stain
slightly smudged
some sort of container
rested there, perhaps—
yes.
a bottle of hair dye
radiant ruby #44
herbal essences, $9.32

*Elie Wiesel (b. 1928), Romanian-born U.S. writer. Quoted in international Herald Tribune (Paris, September 15, 1992)

cherry bomb

like joan jett in black mesh,
she was born doing a cover tune
in your local juke joint for a
quarter slot.

it was cherry bomb,
the first taste of icicle love.
do you wanna touch me?
grinds, riffs in the young hips
on barstools.

the solid 'pop' from cue stick to ball
cocks my radar gun,
and the wild thing was never taught
she wasn't 'sposed to act like that,
talk like that, write like that...

stop when you're ahead, so she often lost
her head...to the heat of the streets on
cool lips pressed like glass blue.
but she'll always belt out a sordid
croon for the love-lorn lost, never
to lay waste to that emotional
gait from the bombshell blonde
to the jett black bet...

always on the longshot
forever on the slip-shot

Cherry Bomb.

hey, kari ann

i'm thankful for sticking to it
for failing
and then winning
the grace of forgiveness
and understanding
when i can't go to the store myself
or you need a washcloth on your neck
for losing it out of both ends

we can laugh
i'm thankful that you now mean it
in the best possible way
when you call me bitch
i'm thankful for taylor swifting
for plastic cars
and inside jokes

p.s.
i'm even thankful when you share stories about _____
because, kid
that means we can share just about anything
i'm thankful for u-gene
honey badger
a million other random things
we have shared
that have made this part of my life
the best.

grandma ham (no relation)

had bottles of cold coke
stored in what resembled a
refrigerator from the
beginning of time
house probably built up around it
made popcorn on the stove
with real butter and
loads of salt

i never knew her when she wasn't an old lady
with a spare room
full of boxes upon boxes
of comic books
casper
archie
richie rich, my favorite
precious treasures
brought out only after
affirmations of good behavior
before i even knew
what bad could be
when all the men were off to somewhere,
i cared not

silly putty
barbie dolls
matchstick cars

i can't remember my bicycle
having training wheels
but i suppose it probably did

she had many sons
and one daughter
with curls, i imagine
tiny hands reaching

another woman raised her
across town
i never knew why
suppose that was the way
sometimes
back then
when shacks grew up
around refrigerators
and indoor plumbing
was a grand addition

if only the boys were
always away
and somebody's grandma
was mine too

all of us
a beat away
from being seen

the winter we were fine

billy is just a man
with a room and a past
he cleaned them both up
tucked them away
to corners
closets
invited me in
for shelter, comfort
i fell in love for that
he didn't need it
or own it
it was enough
to know

visiting woodland palace
—to Fred Francis

the lady and the spider speak
the same language
somehow i miss the note and
shadow passing tins on
the stairs

a flag down meant
in distress
cycle grind white
a poet's book tells me
nothing of
the gun

the things we rely on

follow the sidewalk scratch
the vomit patch outside the local
says good
night, come
again when sam forgets the 86.
the past doesn't matter much
where nobody has
a future

the fields on route 78

when the cities are wiped out
from the terror
and the strikes
backed up from the day
the straw men will
come up
from their grounds
flapping back their wooden doors
creaking limbs, dusting sway
the earth in their hands
all ready with the secret
of re-birth on its tongue
baby fields they'll plant
fat pink rows of them
and cultivate a new,
kinder race, a gentle
soft breed with
purple azure eyes

don't play with me

simple words
not musical
not noisy
but pounding down the street
surprised from a half-sleep at 3am
a-jumping up
and scurry to the window
and peek
like that hard cover book we recite
during christmas caroling time
i'm spreading the horizontal blinds wide
my lights are off
so it's okay

meaningful and full of like, character

i know why sylvia stuck her head in the oven.
if i write them all down, will they go away?
the ear stunt did not suffice—
bloody mess, i bet it was.
it's like an alien source...
...coming from the outside, in;
streaming...

...

...like a beam, steady unkempt—
and one in 50 go somewhere,
then one in 10 go somewhere meaningful.
to what end?
'cause ted left her;
unrequited love brandished the bullet,
as mine holds its strength.
the only word remaining... ...
b
   y
     e

a monologue

i.
...and people run from me
the fiddle player with trunks full
a value i already know, but pay
        flim flam
                   show love
   spread your truth
for what measure
these are cynical times, girl

i'm always talking to myself
  but i can't answer
it is smoke that escapes
        on forced breath
there are lines through piles
of stinking covered regret

ii.
nothing on these keys
     says it like that
   trumpet boy
come blow your horn
one more time
across state lines
i am the girl calling you
call girl calling you
siren sing singing tune
taunting too, to topnotchwitchery
which you grift to me, mack on me
minding not to meddle with the monologue
misinterpret minefields for a dialogue and you're done again

iii.
the clock, girl, your watch
it's off you know, just an instrument
        confidence tricks
    a pigeon drop
i'm no more safe
me o my
to cult
like there ever was a thing
known by that name
these are cynical times, girl

side effects may occur

after all the coffee
and
the cigarettes
vodka
the weed
just to help
tapering off
sleep all the time
sleep none of the time
lose weight
your skin breaks out
and you shake
when the ideas overwhelm
there's lists everywhere
explanations
manifestos, letters
project after project
and poems
you're in love with everything
and everyone (almost)
then it's
kill
them all
burn them down
out of love—of course
or maybe it's manic episodes
and then the other
deep, dark space
that has you wanting
to slit your own throat
those are especially nice
so you cut down on the coffee
even the cigarettes
and try
try

try
to keep up
ride it out
shitting blood
is just a side effect
that's what the pamphlet said
i believe everything
i read in pamphlets

truckers & convicts

that's the dating pool out here
in redneckland
where the meetings
to secede the union
happen the 4th saturday of
every month

east of town

keep staring at my bank account like
one crazy summer and that damn
radio contest
ashtray brimming over and
the slumlord will never know the difference
unless the number don't spike with a
deposit soon

you know the drill?

the therapist says it's
my symptoms
that do it
keep me wrapped this tight
but i say it's the carma bums
and their tales of the open roads
deserted highways
lost generations...
chasing ghosts
like the one i see in my kitchen
or out in the canyon
who knows

when it finally hits i think i'll
go for a drive
east of town
out on the gravel roads
nothing there but the cholla
and a parallel track running train
saying bye for now sweetheart
bye for now

storm

there are forbidden things
that ache at my insides
jump at you
rapture to you
lightning strikes
a spinal chord
a music note
the symphony of
a spring rain
the birds go crazy
afterwards
and the cars are
floating
away

By Plane, Train or Coincidence

west coast notebook entry #9

today we go again.
birds chirping good morning
smoking a bowl on the sidewalk in oakland.
can i turn the hardest criminal to a smile?
i feel sort of naked about it
though it's difficult to imagine
anyone
much pays attention
outside of themselves.

it took a good three months
to figure out
the city.
please just keep on
please just keep keeping
for the various entities
how things get done

for me,
the break
and all the way down
is of no consequence

happy accident

(just here to read the books and hear the stories)

i haven't seen the hollywood walk of fame
disneyland or the chinese theatre
the street names seem familiar
from a movie, maybe
oh that one book
and the neighborhood names
some i know and clearly remember why

i'm told that if i meander down the wrong street
into the wrong section of town
well it won't be good
mexicans with machetes, they said back home
here, the explanation is simply a matter of territory

i'm taken with the history
the struggle
the resilience
and the sadness
that maybe this one little crack in the sidewalk
is all that remains of what once was...

i haven't seen the helicopters circling
or even one hooker of note
the random violence
of which i'm sure is here
as is anywhere else
none of that has happened yet

i saw the hollywood sign from a distance
craning my neck to glance it on a cross street
as we're blowing through this section
to the next
i don't know where i am

or where anything in relation to this is
that, i don't mind so much
sometimes getting lost is preferred
and i love seeing things i certainly didn't expect
but know
i already know
that i could never love driving these streets
and what the natives have forgotten
completely understandable, sure...
still—not everyone dreams of coming to LA.

if only you could bottle it

if all i left him with
was a t-shirt
i'm sorry
the finer points
must have been
well-missed, then

but somehow i doubt it

that entire album
the smell of that one shampoo
and if i can be so bold
a handful of moments
unique but not so rare
in how easy it was
between us

at the tee gee club #1

bob wants to hear metal

we fumble the
quarter
and change the language
to spanish but
eventually he
gets it
three songs later
planet claire
elvis costello
and that one prince song
all the while his fifth wife
and a trip to the philippines

he gets his quarter
time for a smoke
because today the news

and knowing it's coming all along
doesn't grease the wheels for
soundgarden
doesn't temper the pain for
metallica even, old school

iris will watch my drink for me
top it off so i can
say i'm happy
so i can slip and say
i might not be ok

but you know i'll be fine

west coast notebook entry #13
if your process needs a mountain, go

it's very complicated.

possible i might
not come down
from this
highway crest
in the clouds
here comes the rain, just
a sprinkle

one could feel cold
save for the sun-direct
patches of light

you know what it
reminds me of?
as does everything
right now...

when i leave this
mountain
will i leave the memory
of you
here too?

tell me how

west coast notebook entry #23

the air up here though

oh goodness—
these
people
so *faded* to
an alternate
demographic
hiking with starbucks
in american apparel
they brought their own
soundtrack
playing photo shoot
from a boombox in too good
a condition
to make any sense

an insurance commercial
a life stuck
on the share button

these
are genuine smiles
let's post this

as they appear to stand closer
to the edge

you're probably going to worry about the wrong things
like bears or sodomites. so
just don't worry

taking my chances in bear country

remember which hand
you touched the door
with
remember the handi-wipes
next
time
remember that the fires burning
can be either a light to
follow back
or away

the fog rolls in

we're walking in a
cloud now

enough

abundance, it rains
on this sleepy saturday drought
cracks in the sidewalk
and everywhere else
filling up

it was there lurking
clouds heavy with promise
the somber and unrepentant jazz
the lips moments from the kiss
the sweet surrender
that lone trumpet sounding
the all-clear
the alright
with what we already had
right here

west coast notebook entry #4
helicopters don't have blind spots

i can't get a
moment
a patch of sky
a break

i can't get white to
turn black
or vice versa
& they're all out
of grey
can't get a good deal
but i sure
can't get whining
all too much about it

the sprinklers
are on
despite the drought

so many hands
that need washed

and as much as i'd like to
avoid
roundtable discussions
on the politicizing
of a social construct
the city won't quiet
its desperation to manipulate
borders within borders
within borders

studies show
even the helicopters
are in on it

west coast notebook entry #6
when you need to sit in a dark theatre, crying by yourself, with others

you notice it's an everyday thing
you notice it's a three times a day thing
you notice that our last dollars
were maybe more important than all those other dollars
you notice that the kid behind the counter, this one anyway
still smiles in that not in spite of himself way
that us old-timers well that's all we're really wondering about
you notice that when it's over
just enough time was burnt
to cast the perfect shade across the sky
you notice that the city needs more than
a mere spat of rain
to clear the air
& figure maybe
that's how the humans work too

steel reserve 211
high gravity

trading a brown bag beer
from the rite-aid
for a cold
one
in my sweater...
i told you these are
important decisions.
gliding down sunset blvd
when the gradients are just right
the differently-abled humps her walker
at the bus stop
blowing devotions
at the moon sky
& all the while
that twinkle in her eye
a judgment on the navigational
misfortune
of too many things in a day
we are what we wish for hard enough

only in LA, baby
only in LA

west coast notebook entry #27
being so weird at the party

i have to wonder why the heck i'm here
oh you midwestern people,
aren't you so quaint.
oh you writer people,
aren't you so cute
with your angst & rebellion.

i sit next to a daddy gay
& learn about grindr
i'm calling the police at midnight
she screams
so i sneak out
rolling up the hollywood hills
squeezing through those streets
as if anyone could.
feed the feral pussies,
& touch one finger to the moon—
mtv will never be that way again,
neither will i.

west coast notebook re-entry poem #17
vagrant observations

if only all days
were the ways
in which
the rainbow propagates
into jumbo mouse ears.
wrought iron fences shaped to
hold the childhood in.
what sort of wicked porn
turned this into
a busty lustful waterfall moment
a wife-beater
wet w/ sweat moment
an are you joking me
about the avocados moment.
only in the absurd
does absolute purity
dine on skin flick

the center of the country pretends these margins do not exist
while they're ogling all over it
while they're licking the sweat right off

it's an interesting slice of pie

lackluster ending

i need some sunscreen
i need a bag of lemons
i need to hear
a different bird
singing

but st. valentine
delivers none
of these
on this saturday afternoon

a walk in the sun
anyway

i think i'll have a margarita

navy days

ya know,
if you want a sad story,
i've got 'em.
buckets full of guts—
yeah, tarred with cancer.
not your trick,
fine. pass 'round the corner
to the seven guys i fucked for fun
it's not much when you think of seven
certainly not much to my man's 100s
but i'm a gurl.

and boy, he loves to tell them stories
'bout those fuckin' whores he did
back in the navy days
shootin' bananas out their twats
for fuck's sake!

yet i was tender once.
youth had it's way with my head
and a girlfriend too.
well, truth be told
it was mostly just
strawberry fields and electric blankets
but my truth is like mold
in our living room.

so it's all like
yes, cap'n
i'll play the shame
for that one—
in trades for this.

ahead of her class

woke up thinking about a-words
audacity
authenticity

sure sign that winter
will be setting in
soon

amorous
in a room of one's own

afraid (of...)

buscemi

he reminded me of buscemi
and everywhere it was this guy
how i didn't intend it
but i was watching
these random occurrences—well,
seemingly. how could it be that stacked
day on day, unrelated, related
a voice-over, a bit movie part
an old favorite
his cigarette dangles at me
you there, you
and this look-alike
how he was always going when
i was coming
to the grocery
around to the laundromat
i wanted to ask him
do you go cold or
risk the fade

friendly advice

find another way to make money
invent new ways to stalk your lover
start a diet fad
marry a rich man
kill 'em with your good looks
and big tits
don't take a penny
dig graves for a living
with your fierce competitive attitude
sell, sell, sell
aim high
shoot low
find an airfield saturated in hair spray
tell the whole world
about the mood you're in
in other words
lie, lie, lie

as halothane, procaine, or ether

go on with your life
do not become the poem
she will treat you
as an open wound
in a salt factory
mop the floors with you
needle and thread you
without anesthetic
posturing for a picture book
on how you should not do
a fine surgical maneuver
she will make you bleed
a little
enough
just enough to satisfy the page
though, in the end
it will mostly be
pain
for the sake of
pain
you will be left with
question after
question
tripping down the catwalk
under the fluorescent lights
under the footfall of man
day after day
after day
they live the thing you are
knowing not

charlie don't surf!

axl rose is high on moon pies.
   he does frankenstein bits for the pony show.
he confuses manson with the viet cong,
   a chop-shop in the consciousness.
one quarter puts a man's face, flat on a penny.
   i had a summer like that once.
i wore a black hat every day, until
   i left it in the topps big boy;
when they tore it down,
   the fever left me.

who are they

who are the real poets
who are the real people
did they sleep next to me last night
did they tumble from the face of the earth
before i woke
i found a blanket on me
it smelled like lovelies
i only dreamt of a phone call
there was a question
but i forgot why and where
and only this
was left

rules of the road when navigating a trip closet

enter with love
do not snap your fingers
& do not jump out of
the shadows, there is no
need
this is a closet outside
the closet
you are participating
without agenda
be
here

in a moment
we will all spin off
into the universe where rules
are sketchy and
not to be trusted, challenge
your assumptions
this is a safe space
with a pillow to rest
your head
we are
whispering sweet
everythings in your
ear
no permission slip
required, liable
is a funny word

back by sometime still called monday

we travel by landmark and compass
an itinerary that
not only includes
but demands
getting lost

what's needed
is
highly re-evaluated

we have friends in every port—
some will pull through
and some will
forget what day it is

piss by the side of the road
carry various weaponry
but most importantly
always carry a can opener

you do have to know
a stranger when you see one

be careful out there
safe travels, all that

clues to watch out for are:
uniforms.
and anyone else sunk so low
all they have is
it's us or them...
look for desperation
never forget crazy

and anyone thinking they
have/need/are
power.
the bloodlust riffs off them
loud as sirens, those ones

sometimes they come with smiles
but still
you usually know.

how to decide if something is triggering

the sound of a dog slurping water
is triggering
the accidental taste of grit,
triggering.
aqua net hairspray
& grape kool-aid
ruins me
for days.
the crisp
pronunciation
of
names that begin with
the letter C...
fuck, man.
if i had to sit in his lap again
all four years old and trembling,
blacking out in the worst parts—
it would torture and comfort me
for years to come.
well it would not do me any worse
for the detached i have come to learn.
but i love you anyway
and all the
mundane
sights, sounds and smells
that get me on a regular basis / +
a lawnmower in the distance,
the blackened room,
the smell of fresh, boiling
water

xmas shopping list: free hugs, check twice

today i consider my
xmas list
arrange the words in my head
that will explain why
i have no gifts
that will explain why
instead i'm printing up pages
worrying over cover art
regretting that last latte i
didn't need
wondering why i had to go so far
and beg for gas money
wondering why i ever did a fundraiser
to pay for a website
wondering why i gave all those books away
(but i know that one)
why i kept pushing that magical jeep
why i got others to push it with me
i mean, *fuck*
i should have thumbed it
i should have followed the kids
& ran the jug around
stood waiting for the pickup truck
at the day labor
i should have taken up a
corner
and either gone
all-out krishna
or hey, look at my tits!...
just some flesh that will
be gone
in barely a speck-view
of the universe.

my friend has cancer

reject the body.

further
reject the systems
that poison us every. day.
that disinterested glaze
slathered around all that
mind-numbing propaganda
hooked on the divide & conquer
as if television still only comes
in black & white
even the rednecks don't want that anymore

reject any life that is about consuming
to waste
the actual parts that make being a
human
make being alive
make the very air you breathe
in your they set em up you knock em down
doe-eyed slavery
the cutest sheen of
a wonderful life
you'll ever put a hashtag to

kids, i don't know.
i think about all this
think about this community
all those tiny hands full of fight
how life is just too damn hard on people sometimes
how you can't put those hands up to do anything about it
if they're busy holding all those bags

let it go...
hold on only
to what's
important

love you

and go down, in your own way

love is the X factor you can't fuck with

feel more
stockholm
folding into
a space
guaranteed
w/answers

ask questions
i can complicate

the truth is
midnight prayer

you're all a bunch of horrible animals

i come home tonight after many drinks
with friends of like mind
and still i am not consoled
and still i want to google
"how to make a molotov cocktail"
and use one

maybe fear the people like me
with some semblance of how to use the language
to affect
but good luck to anyone counting on that—
i'm not.

if you haven't a two for one special,
fuck off.

they will speak of admiration
and the oh so cute with your revolution
but listen here girlie
there is a better way...

thank you, i am quite practiced
at the grin that gets me through

of all the things i fake upon the universe
this is the worst

i will keep telling my children—yes,
you can. demand it.
i will keep telling the poets, yes—
the world needs you.
the world fucking needs you!

and secretly hate that i am lying.
secretly hate that there is nothing
literally not a thing you can do about it
but rock on with your bad self.
please
please
please
rock on with your bad self.
fuck! if absolution is what you seek,
let me pull out my big white power of knowing what it means
to be an american—the only true
and native son
of an empire set on eating its young.
once again, *god bless us, everyone.*

do not like this post

#i'll tell you why the poets

because i don't want to talk about the weather
because i don't want to talk about the latest episode of
because i don't know my place
because the odometer rolls over and another mile begs
because get outside of yourself, be humbled and exalted at the same time
because ya know, they're tricky
because words do sound better than that when they spin and actually taste
just fine with whiskey
because a good poet and editor will fix that last line
eyedrop of magic
spitshine formaldehyde
because we only get one life to be conscious about
because woke ain't no joke or hipster invention
because i have something to say and those fools on the bus wouldn't listen
because avocado trees and rabid raccoons
because 4am rain
and because i can make coffee anywhere
while the heart stays tuned to that certain beat
i wonder if they know how much i love them
how much i need them
how much the world needs them
christ's sake, the ego—
tell no one, but listen.

you enjoy the privilege of
aka dear white dudes, bite it.

being in the room
presumed innocent
the control of everything

your indignance

the right to look
the right to touch
the right to
  take
    everything
anything your tiny little white male heart
desires

the right to mock

your foot on any neck
credence
authority
your own set of facts

the ease of the world
& the mothered arms of comfort
forgiveness
forbearance

the vulgarity of your denials

rape, pillage, plunder...
women, children,
the meek & disenfranchised

you enjoy it all—
war, genocide, oppression
on a mass and all-encompassing scale

i tell you this
from the safety and comfort
of my own throne of whiteness
blinded by it
every sound of protest a pitiful whimper

do you find it unseemly?

write off the
whore, the heretic,
all simple-minded
well-meaning misunderstandings
of just how
things are
(meant to be)

you enjoy the privilege of
being
the center of the universe
a god
on this planet
across nations
across time
since the dawn of
time itself

with one damn rib
that prick adam
bought the whole enchilada
and it's all yours

i'll wait for you to get it
over here
out of the way
cradling in my bosom
this delicious
red apple.

an accurate description of work yesterday

walked right up to that house full of pit bulls and tiki torches
he's wearing a dress code that can be concealed but today
it's warm &
the full sleeves, profane skin
all the wretched hate on display

how does this happen

smiled as he held the puppy
pleasant, more so than many
am i taller? this can't be
am i growing, is the floor sinking??

i am the most considerate out of body experience
we won't even tell anyone i am smiling
alice? where are you
please help

america, great again

he's not afraid to say nigger

he's not afraid to scream it out the window
across the lawn
and down the way
a serene landscape where no one flinches

he's not afraid to yell it in front of the children
in front of his wife
in front of god almighty and country
knowing fuck-all what it says to the world
let alone, the internal

and still he's spitting hate
like baseball players and chewing tobacco
like fathers beat their children out of duty
out of war-torn memories
collapsed mines
& a nickel in your bucket means anything

tonight your woman dies in a back alley abortion
& the angels rejoice

this is progress.
where you can buy your tiki torches
at the home depot,
armband of the disenfranchised
sold separately

somewhere
baby jesus is weeping

unequalibrium

only going to be responding in code from now on
as is how the universe
speaks to me
do poets we suspect
decipher but what if
we broke
detoxify the lives
can we speak violent, we
don't she
run the line into
a dead end street
your mom had a secret life where
you didn't exist

doppelganger

he reminds me of this boy
if not for a doppelganger, no
reason i would recall
brad, so sullen,
frail &
pissed
drives a 2-seater
and lives
just past that one bend in the road
a little too far out

curious things

i find curious connections
in strings
words
the dog
licking his paws
the way his head moves
bugs
these things make me
love
these things make me
sick

i wonder if i was
born this way
or was it like some
sci-fi movie
rubber-banded from a
corn field
one blank blue night
to a saucer full
of experimenting green men
with round protruding eyes

and...
why are they always men
exploring
while the women sit home
burning the midnight oils

i would burn oils
but anymore
they break them over my head
tell me i can't have a frying pan
in both hands

ladies aren't what they used to be
and the flying man is amused.

drop dead stop

running into drop dead stop—
it hurts, you know.

got a gumption to set myself on fire
but all the signs said "hell no"...
go back the way you came,
so i ended up in that tiny place
droppin' like a damsel, i squirmed
i swore on fate another day
but she found me 'cross the aisle
in that nondescript truck stop
all that brought me was the neon signs
and no car. go, go, go.
not a second of misdirectognition—
but it'd been so long.

where will the story end?
another patron enters, another
messages to atoms, material moves
a plane, i am surely unaware of, working
the road turns, it bows.

silver duct tape

i found a crater in my hand
with your name on it.
i asked where you went,
it said nothing.

there's a new guy here.
he put a wad of gauze there,
lots of tape.
it was silver duct tape,
the kind i fixed my car with.
i was poorer than i am now,
which is not much.
i used to say it could fix anything.
we would laugh,
just laugh our silly heads off.
ha ha ha
ha ha

purchase

it's just past noon on a wednesday
the local gas station buzz
i have a pack of gum
a pack of reds
and a water
the news translates
my secret buried in a tomb
those children there
scurry past and ride off
into the sunset

engaging the dream

that morning
there were
four kittens
on the side of the road
not sure if
they were going
to stay or run
the morning was cold
avoiding last night's
puddles

in step
a mist of rain

you said things
i never wanted
to hear

i see the colors changing
like it's nothing
out of the ordinary

the blue
the very deep blue

the story behind this photo

will it ever be as if he never was?
thought perhaps one of us might
kill the other
in a fit of mad love
or at least so much living
for who dies first

the words are all the life beyond me
i have left to give
and it's just not enough

rather than being accidental

pretty sure the best laid plans
mean nothing
to the sharpie
on your name tag
to the misfitting sweater
and the comes in a package underwear
you are chipped nail polish
broadcast-live
crucifixion
unfiltered by design
the seed of doubt
mother nature uses to
reclaim
the broken
but there is no clean break
there is only sleeping at the wheel
bent
a contortionist running metal
burns one thing for another
the shelves are stocked
with gas ovens
and bottomless drops

take your pick, kitten
your secret is safe
with me

what a fuckin' life, right?

reduced to the
communications
over wires
across time zones

i cannot find
the map
that says

you
are
here.

there'll be time for that later

she began noticing everything
in her world was manilla-
colored. her skin had turned
manilla, the bare mattress on
sheet-changing days...manilla.
the very air filling that room.
yes, manilla. if her life
resembled anything at all, and
perhaps there are more
appropriate words for colors
seen and unseen, but i tell you—
it was every molecule, manilla.

the grainy
the slick
it all tasted the same

she contemplated gold,
soft light,
water shadows,
lampshades.
there is no sound
to manilla

all the laundry turned this color
all the lids
all the unwashed hands
and corners
and every
broken
thing

another layer of understanding

he thought she might be the devil
& she hoped maybe he was/
would be
for those times necessary
only
to take her apart
from the ties that bind
push her farther
onto the edges
where everything
drips
indigo blue...
i know it doesn't make
any sense
but that was
the color
of her
dreams now

thanks for finishing it for me

the filthiness comes so very
naturally
inside his mind
and manifest via text
she is the only thing
that's bad about me
we're so good at delusions
and the long game
think of all the things
between here
and there
before we get caught
in something real

meeting a friend

that first night.

brought in from the rain,
from the dark...
down old highways
over the bridged river.
windows—none,
and county roads
slimmer than one and a half
rugged tires
and fresh bug juice,
a constant current not
the kind that crackles
the kind that maintains.
air thick with it
does not move without
your motion.
cutting through
quite specifically,
navigated
to a bowling alley bar.
you, drunk
in from the chicago train,
already wearing your intended's ring
yet
fresh from a disappointing search
for another.
i suppose you figured
what the hell.
as did i.

step up your gift game with tips from pro wrappers
Bow not included

what do i write anymore
but epic craigslist masterpieces
that get flagged
for being impossible

actionable items only please

the holidays came and went
mourning for the dead
mourning for the living

we eat til it hurts
even if it already did

missed connections
misunderstandings

the world's a mess
but there's always
the clearance aisle

for him

things are rusty
after too much
running
running to
running away
the difference
becomes negligible
after a while

go ahead
& claim
sanctuary

just watch the fuck out
when it decides
to claim
you.

hazard is imminent

there are nine dimensions
of reality
happening
in this space
and time

we are
only three

diving in ocean surf, we
are
warning

multisensory delivery mechanism

in a sense, exact

just keep writing
sensory input
because i'm kind of
at a loss.
glass-encased
seeping heat
space, a bubble
the world turns outside only
twice a day
a snowglobe on a timer
what do we do with this time
as important
as any
oh yea?
there are holes in
the telephone pole out front
maybe a squirrel colony
it's a thin coat of vanilla
frosting
as far as the eye can see
any moment now
you'll be home
home
is that something i'm interested in?
like no other this
makes
perfect sense

tonight i need to let go

but he says
we have to stop
and his plan works
as i feel the disappointment
slide forward, all around
i can't shake it
like that landslide
song
you keep playing
over and over
and over
and you still don't
get the point

until the universe
has decided
i've learned this lesson
well enough

just watch...
the sun rises red
but goes pink early
in the clouds
it doesn't take her long
to be done
look away
and you've
missed it

the choose your own adventure stories we tell ourselves

i'll start doing things
to get out of it—
burning a
hole in your
favorite t-shirt
ruining your
beautiful
record collection...
then i'll remember
the only sound advice
my ex-husband
left me with

you're not required to do
anything in this life,
except die.

all i ever
wanted to write
was a happy ending

how to pull a curtain, no hands
alternatively, closure

when the smell
goes to afterbirth

when the song turns
to shudder

when the bags pack
themselves &

make a run for it
in the middle
of the night

that chapter
is called
goodbye

point of departure

it was february 7th, 2015.
no colder than any days before,
remembered. crisper,
maybe. when there has been snow
and retaining temperatures most often accompanied
by grey days then you get a break like this morning. sun
before the warm reaches and melts a thing, one could look out
over the flattened cornfields of illinois running into the horizon,
the vanilla icing top layer thin that makes that noise when your
shoe pops down to powder and still you might think you could
work up a good slide
and just whoosh off into forever...

this was the point of departure
that would turn into 12 of the 15 states i traveled to in 2015
from february to may.
for the miles,
i'd have to check the record.
admittedly, it was the least anticipated, planned
or organized journey.
just to say that my intention
was to make it count.

you have to stop calling me momma

if only i had a working uterus...
i could birth nations of ____

(and thus begins the problem)

un-gender specifics
breed them sweet
with dirty hands

that smell of lanterns
that smell of lilac falling
common denominator =s beat

chipless wonderers that eat the heads of consumption
the line is too long

the thought is diluted
my babies write poems to burn in a stolen fire
campside, along the cold desert night

not really here today
nor gone tomorrow

if somehow we didn't

have wings that clip
to the black surface
of our waking lives
we might soar
instead of
stutter
at the light
ahead
we might
take that road
into night
unknown
with less trepidation
than ever before

they say
she is not afraid
like it's a bad thing
when they are really bold
they say
she is fearless
in a tone unkind

and quite noticeably
envious

softly i regret to tell you

off in the distance a muffled rumble, close. your eyes. & it.
(do you hear that)
w i l l   v i b r a t e   * t h r u *

don't.
depend.
too hard.
on the adj.
ectives

time is no longer now, fetching for a better view
these babies will be brighter than the rest

our modern dilemma,
the message in the bottle not lost at sea—preserved
forever
and no one

digressing is a
good way to...

will early morning cold always remind me

waking up there
in your body warmth
running downstairs
with the cats to
turn the heat
and the music on

the sun rising
the ease of it all

the clarity

many things

but that
i have not felt
since

plainsong

i am thinking about your place
this cold of winter
this time of day
the sunshine warm
slowly receding
to other glows

years later,
it warms me still.

the extent to which i am floored

off the ground
your love is
too stream of consciousness

isn't it the usual that
fire on a fragile thing
will break

or is it reinforce

what is the most tactile
word you feel
i can't choose between luxurious
& pornographic

you know
when you meet someone who understands
the mechanics of your body
and your mind

i should run
as they say
these things never work out

but today
we meet on the river that
runs contrary to the norm
one of five in the states
says the landlady

the idea

to go beat was the idea
find limits by pushing past
live the art you are going to make
in the decoding process
we all give in

i forgot how to write
& remembered it is just letters
to the best in us willing to listen &
when there's no one there
aren't we forced then
to learn the most

42 trees in a line at this
nutto cement patchwork, anchor-themed retreat
people care here
which is strange for a place
where one goes to be unnoticed

the basics of the superstition
breaking light bulbs 2 at a time

something lost
    something found

how to unbecome

protect your magic
claws
anti-theft planet
(at the end of the
rabbit hole)
       poised

when the road ends
here
this is
where i'll be

putting things where they
belong

unraveling extension cords

sweeping
under the rug

origin of casual
burn this one

the poem where he
meets her
on a bench
at a place
we will never
learn to pronounce
correctly

the walls
drenched in
gasoline—
a lighter
he hands to her.

here you go,
sugar.

burn this one

when he brings me lighters
easy does it with that fire

the non-stop air
is good
setting of alarms
is good
in the mid-day
blues playing
shade drawn
afternoon of him,
life is good.

i barely made it to
presentable,
chores
and nervous energy.
all wasted at the door
as he steps in.

this is the life now
and soon
dinner somewhere
with just the right
breeze
& lighting

to the puzzling situation which seems to involve a contradiction
can i get that martini to go

sitting in the rain
outside the eats
it's too loud
in the bar
with the fancy
people & the
prime rib

i go outside
down the way
to the benches
where nobody sits
with the outstanding
shrubbery & art-
etched sidewalk
that no one notices

the leaves sound off
to another year
all dry and crumbly
going on their way, i
wonder what
the world will mean
tomorrow

the sound of tread on
wet pavement
the smell of winter
coming
of finding a place
to stay for a spell

the other diners shudder by
in their quicksand agenda

i hear the last tale of flip flops
hitting the autumn concrete

it should be a new
moon tonight
the holidays loom
in the next weeks
& we shall see
if all is good

show me

this climate to another
time zone
does the news
& weather report
wreck your hair a different
product placement
at 3am
last week we played
telephone
and the strings
they seared
to your lover's eyebrows
and i
lost in the skydrive
lost in the ether
of words at trainstops

pics or it didn't happen
pics or it didn't happen

at the buffalo

good morning in the still dark

edgy shadows
damp remembrance of yesterday
reporting live from the
drop-in motel
where a combination of
roadside picnics
(comforting if not serene)
& sad domestic situations
occur
simultaneously

expired honey returns
to her room with
package in tow
maybe it's work
maybe it's the kind of work
polite society wouldn't speak of

i keep watch out of the periphery
wonder if the chinese take-out is okay
without refrigeration
it smells like an
alcoholic's wet dream in here
on the margins
but this space in the middle
where it's all warm without a single fuss
where it's all your scent and mine lingered together
on the bed sheets
where the effectiveness of a single yessss
causes the bedside alarm clock to crackle uncontrollably
it's probably responding to some bizarro frequency

i forget your name
i forget mine
it is
the best

if i told you

you wouldn't believe me
so i just poem it

where the sound of
to blur
the voice
reaches cataclysmic
rendering

you know the one
over crackled phone
over a shallow breath
of yet uncalculated risk

if only the lines
curved right
at the
dial tones

a confession
straight ahead

in that all matters complicate and refine

the morning sun +
daybreak's cigarette smoke
fill the room.
his drawers on the floor
where i left them last night

it's been months since
i could even breathe a poem (prayer)
tried communing with those clown car gods—the poets
they had both good & silly things
to say about love, life
and the great & sad state of humanity

i breathe fire, she said
i'll swallow that whole, he replied

ever walk into a bar only to become
witness to an intervention?
the tiniest thing rules the entire room

now the scent of bacon
& gear sounds, shifting on down the road
the waning summer wind already too cold with the lake effect

i'll watch the leaves change from this window

turn in my seat—
i can touch the palm of your foot
i can dwell in the chest of your heart
soft like pudding
or play-doh,
i haven't decided which.

purposeful interaction theory

soon the day comes

in the cold air
now prepped
for a storm
the trucks gathering
anything left not dead
dies soon
& all the whole day is gloom
inside impending clouds
long after the train, the wind
trails gone into
a tunnel
who is to say
how long these signs
are just a pictograph
of curious patterns
and mismatched currents

cityscapes while sitting on a cold, cold stone

it's been a full day
business + reminisce,
lake shore & shoreline.
the city...
it costs to walk the streets here.
unnoticed is unpaid...
not everyone has a dream beyond
a warm meal and a safe bed.

street gospel thaws a pedestrian
every 6 or 7 turns.
that's not too bad
but it's not too good either.

can you tell me where the yellow brick road goes
when unaccompanied by
red sequined shoes?

there is a home in the heart of
every traveler, she thinks
as he walks away
pretending
to save her number
& she knows
& she smiles relief
to the tips
of her
toes

found mister d #7
gas station dialogue

no problem—
have a good night
tires are washed out
clutch is sticking
dr pepper, not much
else is clicking
their dad needs his lotto cards
pays with a roll of quarters
he goes back in one more time
the sixth

the winter wears on

i'm getting fat
& you
are getting mean
there is no
dog to hunt
or even sleep
at the foot of the bed
there lies only
a dream

when will the sun shine again

but he don't know what it means

it appears like nagging
this unrestrained desire for more
give me
give   me
give
    me

the setting is a room
with soft white walls
a flowered plant in various
stages of bloom, charming in all
from ripe to waning...
fresh air, billowing
the curtains into your space,
knocking things over and
snuffing out the candlelight

if one could direct the flow of energy
would not one shut the fucking window?

love

soon my teeth will fall out
and the broken glass on the floor
will get cleaned up
how on earth can a mind be unrest
while dealing in such certainties
i walk the dogs
i prepare a meal
things are folded with nary a thought
i'll cradle this one little word until i die
even if it kills me

walk in your shoes, boy

you bought them

they are all so pretty
and waiting
just
for you

game over

why can't we just be friends?

why can't i just continue to put my penis in you?

why can't you exist in a sphere with no emotions?

why can't you just be my mommy?

why can't you just take it, hard?

> *harder?*

why can't you just let me take care of you?

why can't you just need me all the time for everything but actually not too much?

why can't you forget the weight of a word like love?

why can't you suspend truth?

> let's play.

the science of breaking up
taken down by you

removed from the planted feet
on shaken ground
but i was at steady
and there you are with your pinholes
irrational, sweet little desires
that they are
a worked-over poem can be good
but can it be honest
i wish i could speak of the stars
or a hummingbird, landing it fierce
and new on your ears, still
saying something...
weighty.
the words would be of sinew, sinewy
and yet there is no meat
a connected emptiness, related
this dissipated space to the next
don't you know you fall through such tangles?
don't you know nothin' at all

when she figures out it's not a love story—
love story resolutions

let her go.

regret is for the
moon dust
she leaves behind
somewhere there
in the days you spent

akin to the last rays
at sunset
to the kiss
that lingered
longer than it lasted...

simple question

i loved him as much as he would let me
how much does this heart weigh now

imposterization

the city creeps
the night screams
it's all so noir
and smudgy—

stand next to something
real, maybe
you are
projecting

maybe somewhere else
but not here
the city here gnaws on itself
the only sound you hear is
look who's over there...
look who's looking
look

porch sessions #1

i am the tired of bones
tossed at sea &
washed up in a nether land

i should find what makes for bones
or become an adornment
or a pulverized mix of things
meant for something special and mysterious...

like love
oh love
oblivious to coercion
does it wait on untended beaches
for washed-up things?

destiny is the trust of waves
and do you know what that looks like?

while thinking about all those suicidal adults
and your own relative story
porch sessions #2: survey

pause
for a moment
focus on the why
a 2 month old child
might be referred to
cps.

an acronym meaning
fucked
from the get-go.

you think i sell them short?
i don't.

some are mistaken
and some will
pull through anyway,
some
    how

pull that focus back in
((*see the baby*))

cradle their head in your hands
check the head circumference.
do the eyes follow the light?
the sound of your voice?
when you stretch out those little legs,
how far do they go?
can you measure their weight
in your arms?
step onto the scale
& tell me.

check once,
twice,
three times...

this assessment will be over in approximately
90 minutes.

that's really all the time we have
thank you for your input

a number of various things today
porch sessions #3

watched a flower slowly bloom
from the front porch
it takes a long time
it's still not done
i felt, once again,
the blooming of heartache
surround my lungs
and settle in.

it takes a long time
it's still not done

quietly destructive things
a person whom the speaker dislikes or despises

is how i get fat and bad haircuts
is how bad men
"get" me

examinations

thank you
for the tiny metal implements, sharp
digging into torn flesh
furrow out black misshapen bits of rock
gravel lodged in various degrees like maggots
burrowing deep

are you pregnant with it
bleeding no part
now i walk this path
my own
wounds wrapped
tight like oats, thick.
come in capsules. why
do we
come in veils

spacetime continuum for dummies

it took me five days
to realize why i was
so depressed
the anniversary
of the day we met
some years ago, now
different everything

i didn't notice the date...
keep track of the day of week
by what everyone else
around me
is doing

soon there'll be
a new anniversary
though i forget the date
the last time i saw you

we'd spent the night
in a white trash
ghetto
airbnb
played pool for most the hours
set a grill on fire
pretended to fish
i washed the dishes
and after
we just laid there
talking quietly
about the times
good, bad, and ugly
holding hands
like a couple of junior high kids
tick of clock

tick
tick
tick

in the morning
we did not say goodbye

we had a fit
like no other,
a love affair
to match

i guess
that'll have to
be enough

Prose Poems

Dear Raving Lunatic

Dear Raving Lunatic,

Check your manual for citations, denote and intone only serial libations for we are set off on a cycle of impressive rotation. Jam your head gear with the finest in meditations, color me quasi-stimulated, else I pass the moral compass, put you off with such a rumpus...dear, I really can't be clearer on just how we have got here. STOP!

Now, if I could be so bold—an incantation, you'll see the relation, to the cold that's burning through your veins in a coagulating fit. Though, nothing has transgressed in which the sinner cannot press into the bosom of our friendship fold for fold.

In the lines of black and white from that mirror all cracked and slight, a joker and a pawn, we've come so far, so long...a misfortune has been incited to the tune it must be righted. Dance the middle ground to spare, sing a long lost brother's hail, get with all your best devices, bring out all your verses in justice...to entwine us, trust us, to meander down the path to sound, a most lovely thought so ever found.

Faithfully Yours,
The Girl Underground

One Shot to the Eye

Out of fifty-one pages, I find ten that have eyes. Doesn't that seem strange? Then I go to looking at those masters of university journals—those ones with PHDs and long bios behind their names. It's a faux pas, you see. Though I get the gander, every time. I spread them out like alphabet soup, to find a ghastly amount of bird feathers: birds in trees, birds on my window sill, caws, crows, blue jays on branches...bickering? Then she takes the little white boy down to the church, puts him with the wise old black man...spit and polish, words on spit and polish. In the next line, she does dare allude to sex and misdeeds, speaking in tongues. I'll give her eyes for that. I'd blow out my skull to save one page another mockingbird song and dance.

String Theory

I have been completely mistaken for that which has remained viable, and any sense of what was a reasonable suggestion, or rather explanation of what makes this whole thing map out into any type of equation.

     On Route 66, it was Eisenhower's youth dream—a gathering of troops.
We had extensive, wound-out talks
     (at times reaching scandalous proportions)
Amongst the best of us—at least we felt we were, but America saw on those highways, numbered 2000+ miles, plaster Dinosaurs—roadside attractions, yet at the time, We, of self-appointed importance—committed
     to a common Mission of decisiveness, a cohesive mind range, upon that wave-length is where the hypothesis was born. Many miles had been traveled;
(past, to arrive to this place, then another and another
(all completely, utterly, ridiculously coincidentally linear))
thus converging at the event, little Bobby knew.
     Relatively speaking, he had plenty of the Fourth Dimension.
It surely felt the essence of life, the very dawning of our brilliant scope of all things, Juxtaposition Grandeur—A Purple Giant.

Nothing felt heavy-handed nor presumptuous, certainly not licentious.
I would not have stood for it. So, one by one, it all came together,
this outer-limits, wonder-fulfillment genius, that now unravels, which
just proves and un-proves itself false and true.

"Bobby—what do you see, son? (from the eyes, the great big, empty eyes of the soul-less relic) "...looks like sandfights, Dad! All I can see is sandfights!"

Aren't we all just connected by strings—like everything?
Supergalactic, round balls of string—
multiplying, unifying everything!

It was movies with catchy names like *Twister* that got your eye. They had trucks with cabs that chased, watched as the tornadoes did what came naturally, lopped-off the head of that beloved purple rex. There are parts of 66, decommissioned, dying breeds—roads that begin and end   nowhere.

It would be advised, We thought, let loose of granules, sinking holes they become, when gathered. Though pitted now, at war, we saw the same desert floor. Bobby's vantage point did not impart this nugget of sphere reckoning, not simultaneous

        ...like the five at Slaughter's House, he leapt, looped—forward, back, and again—strung on a string of electric paradox.

A necessity for connectivity before reaching the end of the line as spoken by the Roadhouse Blues Man—was ever so clear. There you find the remnants of a natural condition meets man-made vision, where Bobby awaits the Return...
        lopped-off head, and all. A life's blood spent on the riders of the storm must know by words to follow, thus we parted with our wine to find these truths.

I have been completely mistaken for that which has remained viable, and any sense of what was a reasonable suggestion or rather explanation of what makes this whole thing map out into any type of equation.

Like Fingertips in Hallways

It's the coincidence that pulls her to the window on the night of a full moon, just to draw a smile from her eyes, a nod of acknowledgment from that secret place. As dusty as the idea is, it is the revolution of past deeds, the tremor of a path diverged.

It's all about howling at the moon.

It's her, sittin' on the porch of her nice family home, listening to Cardinals baseball on the radio with her husband, while the dog sits at their feet. The three kids are runnin' round the yard, chasin' after lightnin' bugs, and she's content. She really is.

It's that one tattoo she has. If you look closely at her hand, you can see it on her ring finger. She'll never get another, not because it hurt...she actually found it kind of thrilling, but because another would cheapen the one she has.

It's in the stone of that ring, the symbol that is the Yin Yang, the symbol of the stark differences between her husband and herself; the way they fit together.

But it also represents her. The constant struggle she finds within herself. All of the outside bearings that say 'This is, and should be,' and what she feels is her natural language.

Why write about it? It's certainly not a struggle exclusive to her. Shit, man. If you can find somebody who says they aren't tempted by something, they're lyin'.

So, while she finds the greatest part of her resting in ease, so many nights, just porch-sitting, the crackle of the radio and burn of citronella oil enough to entertain her thoughts...

...there's this moon tonight, this larger-lookin-than-usual, big, bright orange moon, and she remembers when she would raze the night to this moon.

And somewhere back there, a different woman stirs. She took a different road and we only see each other on nights like this— like fingertips in hallways.

So, I just want to tell her "It's okay. Me and the moon, we're alright."

If she needs to reach us, she knows where to look.

When Progress Is Working Your Way Back

The call came at a time of quiet panic, days of vinyl, solitude and warmth. Turns out you can panic anywhere. Faced with being stuck in a witness booth, a glass case—out of harm's way but in the thick of it, just the same. Recording the events with heartbreaking precision. The most recent undoing, detached and yet tethered to another wreck. Doesn't matter at that point if I caused it or not, past tipping and yet unsunk is no time to get analytical about it. "Actionable items only" is the mantra of the survivor. So the timing was perfect for that call...

Pristine Settings

We can sleep with the doors open to the LA air despite the smoggy edges probably worse for us than we realize. Still, there is that energy. Maybe it's the how and why of what we find viable. Every man gets lost not to himself but to some collective. It feels like strength yet it is of another. Today I get lost with the day of korean shopping malls. The bathrooms are good but I am fat in this world, if it matters.

Just Some Mushy Shit

Dreaming of your arms but woke up freezing. Into all the unspoken, in every language that there is—love is both the easiest and hardest to translate. *Il mio amore,* such missness. Sleep more now in my coat. Maybe I need to reconsider my substitutions.

Magical Thinking 101

If I was at home where I belonged, I'd be taking a nap right now. I'd have let the record player blare into nothingness but a faint swish, swish, swish. I might wake up feeling a bit lazy and a lot contented, switch to an old CD and swipe the counters and tables and whatnots of dust real quick before you're due home. If the house had grown cold, I'd make it warm again...tending to the unlit fires as if I had a say in it.

MICHELE MCDANNOLD has organized poetry events and/or performed poetry with a bunch of unabashed free-thinkers across this great United States, most happily by roadtrip but sometimes by plane, train or coincidence. She spends most of her time producing and publishing books, when she's not out killing miles with her magical jeep. Michele is the founder of The Literary Underground, Roadside Press, and Citizens for Decent Literature Press.

MORE ROADSIDE PRESS TITLES

MORE ROADSIDE PRESS TITLES

MORE ROADSIDE PRESS TITLES

Perseverance:
The Making of a Musician
Steven Grey

The People Are Like
Wolves to Me
William Taylor Jr.

Fatherless Children
Michael D. Grover

The Work Anxiety Poems
Alan Catlin

A Better Loser
Nathan Graziano